First Published in 2007 by Victory Belt Publishing.

ISBN 10: 0-9777315-6-1
ISBN 13: 978-0-9777315-6-5

This book is for educational purposes. The publisher and authors of this instructional book are not responsible in any manner whatsoever for any adverse effects arising directly or indirectly as a result of the information provided in this book. If not practiced safely and with caution, martial arts can be dangerous to you and to others. It is important to consult with a professional martial arts instructor before beginning training. It is also very important to consult with a physician prior to training due to the intense and strenuous nature of the techniques in this book.

Cover by Diablo Valley Design and Fly Studios

Printed in China

MIXED MARTIAL ARTS
THE BOOK OF KNOWLEDGE

BJ PENN

WITH GLEN CORDOZA & ERICH KRAUSS

PHOTOGRAPHY BY GLEN CORDOZA

VICTORY BELT PUBLISHING

CALIFORNIA

WWW.VICTORYBELT.COM

CONTENTS

The Ground Game

FIGHTING FROM THE DOWNED GUARD

GUARD TOP

GUARD BOTTOM

THE BACK

ABOUT THIS BOOK

The aim of this book is not to teach all of the techniques from each of the disciplines involved in mixed martial arts competition. Such a goal would be virtually impossible in anything under ten thousand pages. It also wouldn't be a book on mixed martial arts. Success in the sport is not based upon how many techniques you know from the striking arts and the grappling arts, but rather how well you can blend essential techniques from the different arts together. As a result, that's what we focused on in the following pages. Meshing techniques from Brazilian Jiu-Jitsu, kickboxing, and wrestling, this book offers a complete mixed martial arts system that both beginners and experienced practitioners can follow.

I've included the techniques that have worked time and again for me throughout the years in competition, but by no means should you stop with what you find here. There are an endless number of ways to blend the striking and grappling aspects of the sport, and you should experiment as much as possible. The sooner you discover what works best for you, the quicker you will rise toward the top of the MMA mountain.

Special thanks goes out to the entire Penn family for helping out with this project, treating the Victory Belt Staff like family, and being so utterly generous. This project is also indebted to Dave Camarillo, Siegfried Krauss, Merrelin Krauss, Mike and Lisa Cordoza, Raffi Nahabedian, Eric Hendrikx, Orion Star, Robb Wolf, and all of the training partners who gave up days of their time for the photo shoots.

INTRODUCTION

Just Scrap

At the age of seventeen, I spent the majority of afternoons in my backyard with a group of friends. We would throw on some old, ratty gloves and take turns boxing each other senseless well into the evening. It was during one of these sparring sessions that we caught the attention of a man named Tom Callos, who had moved in six or seven houses down. He was a tae kwon do instructor who had taken some jiu-jitsu lessons from Ralph Gracie when he was out in California. He loved the little bit of groundwork he had acquired, but the problem was he didn't have anyone to roll with in our small town of Hilo on the big island of Hawaii. Discovering that I was always boxing at the house, he thought I would be a perfect candidate.

I was instantly turned off the first time he came to the house and asked if I wanted to do some training on the wrestling mats. I didn't have a great understanding of what jiu-jitsu entailed, but I ignorantly thought any form of combat that took place on padding had to be a waste of time. My only desire was to train techniques that worked in the street, so I made up some kind of excuse as to why I couldn't train with him. Tom went away, and I thought that would be the end of it. But then he came back and talked to my father. My father talked to me, and I made up another excuse. Turning Tom down twice should have done the trick, but he came again and again. Eventually my father pulled me aside.

"If you don't go, this guy won't leave me alone," my father said. "You have to go train with him one time, and then you never have to go again."

I bit the bullet for my father and went to train with Tom, thinking it would be a huge waste of time. Although I knew absolutely nothing about grappling, I was convinced that I would clean the mat with him. That's not the way things played out. He caught me in an arm bar and then a choke and then another arm bar. It ruffled my feathers a little, but even more than that, it made me curious. Boxing was all about knocking your opponent into oblivion, but jiu-jitsu was about using controlled movements and your opponent's reaction to those movements to manipulate him into a submission. It seemed that with good grappling skills you could make your opponent feel as helpless as the day he was born, and that just wasn't possible in boxing. You could bloody your opponent up and put him to sleep in boxing, but no matter how in control you felt, your opponent still had a puncher's chance.

Needless to say, I was hooked. Tom no longer needed to drop by the house and pester me to come train. I met him every day on the wrestling mats. I still didn't think that jiu-jitsu was designed for the street, but it had certainly snared my attention.

A large part of the reason I liked it was that the sport came naturally to me. The techniques and set-ups just made sense, and I had an instant advantage due to my natural flexibility. With some effort, I was soon able to catch Tom with the techniques he had used to catch me. He enjoyed watching me excel under his instruction, but he also knew that in order for me to truly dig into the discipline, I would need to train with someone who had a more in-depth understanding of it.

Not long after we started rolling, Tom planned a trip to California to test for his black belt in tae kwon do. He was going to be right down the street from Ralph Gracie's academy, and he thought I might like to get a taste of what advanced jiu-jitsu practitioners could do. I was cocky like most sixteen-year-old kids, primarily because I had yet to be humbled, but that all changed when I took Tom up on his offer and climbed onto the mats with some of Ralph Gracie's students.

Within ten minutes it became very clear to me that I had a long way to go before I could even consider myself a moderately decent jiu-jitsu player. I thought I had gotten pretty much tooled at every turn, but I guess I didn't do quite as poorly as I'd thought. Ralph told Tom that I had a future in the sport, and when we got back to the big island, Tom relayed this information to my father. I saw the compliment as just that, a compliment. My father saw it as a whole lot more.

At the time, I was spending a considerable amount of time hanging out with my friends at the beach. I had no direction, and my father was concerned. He thought it would be good if I got off the island for a spell, but where to send me presented a problem. When he heard that I had talent for jiu-jitsu, it solved that problem. By sending me to California to train, I would not only be getting away from the late nights and street fights, but I would also be doing something constructive that took drive and determination. I would be doing something to better myself.

I was against the idea because I loved the haphazard life I had created in Hilo, and I didn't want to leave the festivities on the beach behind. It turned into quite a battle, but eventually we settled on a compromise. I would be allowed to continue with my life in Hilo for six months, but when those six months were up, I would make the move to California.

I was seventeen at the time, and six months seemed like an eternity. I agreed to the terms because I thought that day would never arrive. When it did, my father stuck to his guns. Boarding the plane I wanted to cry. I figured my life was pretty much ruined.

It was rough in the beginning. I lived a bike ride from Ralph's Academy in Pleasant Hill, California. Getting used to the fast-paced nature of the big city after growing up on an island where everything happens slow was one thing, but trying to adjust to an environment where I had no friends or waves to catch was another matter entirely. I got insanely bored, and the only thing I could do to quench that boredom was train.

I peddled down to Ralph's twice a day, everyday. I realize most of you reading this book would probably kill for such an opportunity, but at that time jiu-jitsu wasn't as mainstream as it is now. I had no idea that you could make a career out of grappling. All I knew was that I was bored out of my mind with no one to cruise with.

My main goal was still to become the best fighter out there, but I didn't yet see jiu-jitsu as the ultimate discipline for the street. It relied heavily upon the gi, and no one I had paired up with in the street had ever worn a gi. As a result, I trained without a gi whenever I had a chance.

In an attempt to sway me over to the traditional route, a couple of guys I trained with showed me a tape of jiu-jitsu competition. I suppose the idea was to get my blood pumping from the highly competitive nature of a jiu-jitsu tournament, but at the time I was still so obsessed with striking and knockouts, I missed the point entirely.

The boredom was what caused me to enter my first competition as a white belt. I had been earning more and more taps over my training partners, and Ralph wanted to see me compete. Not thinking much of it, I went to the event, threw on my gi, and climbed onto the mats. I must have been out there for less than a minute when I felt this fire well up inside of me. My mind turned off, and everything washed away except for my jiu-jitsu. I knew it wasn't a street fight, but it was still a fight. I gave everything I

had, and by the end of the day I had defeated all of my opponents in my division, as well as all of my opponents in the open white-belt division. I entered the tournament certain it would be a long, drawn-out day, and I left feeling the most excitement I'd had since coming to California.

Wanting more of that fire and excitement, I entered Joe Moreira's Blue Belt International not long after. Although I was still a white belt, I managed to defeat all of my blue belt opponents. They were obviously of much higher caliber than what I had experienced in the first tournament, and I started getting the feel for what a jiu-jitsu tournament was all about. It was about the competition. The will to win. Stringing together the techniques you've been learning from day to day to form a science. It was about shedding the future and the past so that nothing mattered but the moment. It was about all these things, and I absolutely loved it.

As one competition led to another, it didn't take long for the appeal to turn into obsession. Jiu-jitsu became all I could think about. I thought about it when eating, when taking a shower, when walking down the street. I would have dreams about strangling my opponents. In a way, jiu-jitsu started to drive me crazy because I couldn't get the techniques and set-ups out of my head, not even for a moment. Realizing my only hope of expelling the discipline from my mind was to master it to the best of my ability, I put all of my focus into training.

Three and a half years after I began, I received my black belt. I had competed in a large number of tournaments by that point, so I flew down to Brazil and entered the Brazilian Jiu-Jitsu World Championships, the Mundials. I didn't have any preconceived notions as far as how I would do going in, but when I made it to the finals I came to a profound conclusion. I was sitting down having lunch with a friend, and he informed me of just how monumental winning the Mundials would be. It started to sink in, and I told myself right then that I didn't care if my opponent broke my arm or leg or back. I was going to do whatever it took to win.

When I boarded the plane to head back to California, I was the first non-Brazilian in history to have won the Brazilian Jiu-Jitsu World Championships.

MMA

A short while later, I sat down and tried to decide where to go next. I was twenty years old and still had a lot I wanted to accomplish in grappling, but I also wanted to explore real fighting. As it turned out, there was a perfect medium to utilize them both—The Ultimate Fighting Championship. I had dabbled in MMA training over the years, even entered an MMA competition when I was eighteen. I knew I would have a pretty big leg up over my opponents when it came to grappling, but I also understood that you could not win an MMA fight on grappling alone, especially when you were competing against the best fighters in the world. The main hole in my game had to do with bringing the fight to the ground. In jiu-jitsu, I had never learned any takedowns.

Understanding that wrestling was as technical in the takedown department as jiu-jitsu was in the submission department, I began training with as many wrestlers and MMA fighters as I could. In addition to picking up a whole slew of takedowns, I also learned little tricks on how to blend those takedowns with both striking and submissions.

I cannot express in words how much branching out helped me. I truly believe that you can learn something from everybody, whether that somebody is a white belt or a black belt. Some of the techniques and strategies you acquire will fit nicely into your game, and others won't suit you at all. But it is extremely beneficial to keep an open mind and absorb what you can from people who are willing to share. If you only train in one place, you only have one idea.

One of the MMA fighters that I learned from was UFC veteran John Lewis. In addition to being a wealth of knowledge, he was also very well connected in the MMA world. Before long I found myself rolling with UFC president Dana White at Lewis' academy in Las Vegas. Although White witnessed my skills on the mat firsthand, he was a little skeptical of allowing me into the event. This was beyond the days when you could beat an opponent with jiu-jitsu alone. Every opponent was now versed in jiu-jitsu, as well as versed in how to defend against submissions. In order to win a fight, you had to know everything—striking, wrestling, and jiu-jitsu. White saw me as a strict jiu-jitsu guy, not realizing I had been scrapping all of my life.

He eventually decided to give me a chance, and on May 4, 2001, I found myself standing in the locker room backstage, preparing for the long walk down to the Octagon where I would do battle with Joey Gilbert, an experienced wrestler and MMA fighter. I remember gazing into the bathroom mirror, and it felt like I had stepped away from myself. I knew I was facing a different kind of challenge than I had experienced in jiu-jitsu tournaments. In jiu-jitsu, you can win with skill. In a fight, you have to win with your heart and mind. You still have to be skilled, but if you don't have that fire in your eyes, your opponent will walk right through you.

Under normal circumstances I'm quiet and reserved, but that night in the locker room I stepped outside of myself. The only thing on my mind was victory.

In the first few seconds of the first round, I moved toward my opponent and let him have it with my hands, just as I had done countless times with opponents on the streets of Hilo. But instead of trying to finish him off on my feet, I used my strikes to help me bring the fight to the ground. Once there, I battered Gilbert around, took his back, and flattened him out belly-down on the canvas. I unleashed with punches to the side of his head, and a few moments later the referee intervened.

I can honestly say that was the most important fight of my life. There was no belt on the line, but it was the first time I had fought in front of that many people. Listening to the music and the cheers of those in attendance ran a chill up and down my body. I had just lost my MMA virginity, and I knew I would never experience a moment like that again. I had discovered my destiny, the place I belonged, and I realized I would be involved in the sport in some fashion for a long time. The title belt still lurked far off in the distance, but after that first bout I decided it was only a matter of time until I wore that shiny piece of metal around my waist.

I carried that determination into my next fight against Din Thomas, the number three ranked lightweight MMA fighter in the world at the time. I knocked him out with a knee to the jaw in less than three minutes. Later that year I knocked out the always-dangerous Caol Uno in just eleven seconds.

Having three lightning-fast victories over top contenders in a very short period of time did wonders for my popularity, but it did little to prepare me for a long, drawn-out battle in the Octagon. And I knew such a battle was in store. Winning three fights in a row didn't make me feel invincible. It made me feel as though I had a lucky star following me around. I knew enough about lucky stars to realize that they could be there one minute and nowhere in sight the next.

After just three fights in the Octagon, UFC management gave me a shot at Jens Pulver and the lightweight title. Pulver was an exceptional wrestler with great punches, but I knew that I could beat him. I trained hard, just as I had for my past three fights. In the back of my mind, I realized that I should probably change my training routine up a little, make some refinements so I could keep improving. The problem was I didn't yet know what needed improving. When you lose a fight, you get to see the holes in your game that seldom become apparent through victory. Since I hadn't lost a fight, I didn't see the holes.

I handled that bout just as I had my past three—as a street fight. I was hopped up on adrenaline the entire time. Such a strategy worked wonderfully in my first battles because they came to such a quick conclusion, but Pulver managed to hang on through my first round attempts to put him away.

At the end of the first round, I ran back to my corner, unnecessarily burning energy, but then at the beginning of the second, I had a difficult time getting my momentum going again. It was quite discouraging, but the bottom line is that no fighter can get to the top without paying his dues, and at that point I hadn't paid my dues. If you had added up all the seconds I had spent in the Octagon before that night, it might have totaled two rounds. I needed ring experience to learn all the intricacies of competing in a five round war. My nerves and lack of experience wore on me, and as a result Jens took home the decision. That night he was a seasoned MMA veteran who fought a terrific fight.

Although losing the decision hurt, I'm glad that things played out as they did. If I had won, I would have retired from MMA that very night. That was my plan—get the belt and retire. Coming out of battle in defeat motivated me to better myself and my game. I realized that an MMA bout was nothing like a street fight or a jiu-jitsu match because it consisted of rounds, and anytime there are rounds, you have to pace yourself. I needed to learn how to deal with the constant stopping and starting, and the only way I could manage that was by handling my training and matches less like a street fight and more like a sport. Once I realized this, I became determined to do whatever it took in training to fight the perfect fight.

After a lot of hard work, I started my second run for the title belt strong, earning a TKO over Paul Creighton in UFC 37, but then my momentum slowed. I earned a decision over Matt Serra and then I had a draw with Caol Uno. Both fights were disappointing because I knew I hadn't performed up to my ability. I had wanted so bad for my fights to be perfect, yet neither one came even close to that. The draw with Uno got me down. I thought a lot about retirement. I took a step away from training to find my bearings, but the motivation to return to the sport didn't materialize.

Deep into my hiatus, I decided to pop my fight with Joey Gilbert into the VCR while sitting on the couch one day. I didn't care much about fighting at that point, so it was more out of boredom than anything else. When I saw myself in action, it was as if I were looking at someone else. I couldn't believe the fire that I'd had. I realized then that by trying to do everything perfect, I had lost the drive that had allowed me to win those first fights with such ease.

I had been on an impossible mission. No one can fight the perfect fight. Fighting is pure chaos, and to be a good fighter you simply have to be mentally and physically prepared to handle that chaos. Stepping away from the scrapper mentality to improve upon my skills had been a necessary step to learn all the intricacies of MMA competition, but now that I had improved upon my skills, it was just as necessary for me to reacquire that unbridled aggression. It was time to come full circle.

Looking back, I feel extremely lucky to have popped

that tape into the VCR because it told me exactly what I needed to do. Maybe it was fate, I don't know. But something changed inside of me.

With my head right again, I reacquired the fire and brought that rawness into my next bout with Takanori Gomi, which took place on the big island in my brother's Rumble on the Rock fight organization. I attacked him as a scrapper with skills, and submitted him with a rear naked choke in the third round. Seeing how dangerous my newfound skills could be when blended with my passion and aggression gave me all the confidence in the world. I felt ready to do what I had set out to do when I first entered MMA competition—claim a UFC championship belt.

I took the first opportunity I could get, and it just so happened that that opportunity was for the welterweight title, not the lightweight title. Instead of fighting Jens Pulver, I would be taking on Matt Hughes. I understood that Hughes was one of the greatest champions to ever grace the Octagon, but that mattered little to me. I had found a sense of direction, both in fighting and my personal life. Nothing would get in my way.

I trained like an animal, and when I stepped into the cage that night, I knew without a doubt that when all was said and done I would have the title belt wrapped around my waist. I knew it could be a rough fight, and that I might get cut and head home bloody, but there was no question as far as who would be victorious. While training for the fight I kept an open mind, adapted to changes in the sport, and maintained unrelenting determination. Such a combination is a recipe for success.

I held fast to my game plan, which was to pummel Hughes with strikes and then use jiu-jitsu to take him out. Capitalizing on the first mistake Hughes made, I put him on his back. Once there, I immediately started dropping hard strikes to set up my passes, as well as using my passes to set up hard strikes (a strategy I thoroughly lay out in the following pages). Hughes managed to defend quite well for a few moments, but because I was throwing so much at him, I eventually created an opening to land that one hard shot that rocked him. While he was dazed and confused, I passed his guard, took his back, and locked in a rear naked choke. A few minutes later, I had the UFC title belt wrapped around my waist.

Full Circle

After achieving my ultimate goal in the UFC, I decided to branch out and achieve some other goals I had in MMA, primarily competing in Japan. I knew this might result in losing the UFC title belt, but a belt is just a belt. No one could ever take away that moment. As they say, a memory lasts a lifetime.

In May 2004, I flew to Japan and did battle with Duane

Ludwig, one of the best strikers in MMA. To bring the fight to the ground, I stepped forward with a left hook and then transitioned right into a double-leg takedown, which is one of the first combinations I show in this book. Having trained jiu-jitsu since the age of seventeen, I pretty much had my way with him on the ground. I claimed the mount, transitioned into the kata-gatame choke (p. 265), and finished the fight

My next fight was back in Hawaii with Rodrigo Gracie. I knew this would be a good fight for the fans—the local boy against the up-and-coming Gracie. He was a lot bigger and stronger than most of the Gracie fighters, but by this point I was very confident in my direction and MMA game. Rodrigo might have been a large fighter with a tremendous amount of skill, but I knew that by blending my strikes with takedowns, as well as blending my striking with passes and submissions, I had a lot of ways to earn the victory. Rodrigo was also an excellent mixed martial artist, but he hadn't truly bolstered his jiu-jitsu with other aspects of the game. Such a style doesn't make you a bad fighter, it just limits your options.

On the night of the fight I attacked him with strikes and wrestling, which definitely helped earn me points on the judges' scorecards, but what allowed me to defeat him was superior jiu-jitsu.

Shortly after that fight, I entered the K-1 fighting organization in Japan. The promoters threw some names around for my first opponent, and one of those names happened to be Ryoto Machida. I knew he was a very large fighter—two hundred and thirty five pounds to be exact—but I was excited to see how my skills fared against an opponent who grossly outweighed me. I wanted to test myself, and it turned out to be quite the test. Machida punched like a mule and kicked even harder.

Although I backed him up with punches for most of the fight, he did an excellent job sporadically pinning me up against the ropes and holding me down on the ground, earning points. I lost by decision, but I learned a lot from that fight and feel that if we were to meet again, the outcome would be much different.

To build my name in the K-1 organization, I took on Renzo Gracie when the event came to Hawaii. I didn't take the fight lightly, but I didn't train as hard as I had for a lot of other fights. Renzo turned out to be one tough S.O.B. He executed a handful of techniques throughout the course of battle that caught me by surprise and annoyed me, several of which I adopted and included in this book. The way I earned the victory was by blending the striking and grappling aspects of the sport, as well as outdoing him with jiu-jitsu. As I will mention many times throughout this book, it is best to rely primarily upon your base discipline when fighting. My primary base is jiu-jitsu, so that is what I focus on. I add in striking and takedowns to make

my jiu-jitsu better, but I generally don't steer too far from the familiar.

After four fights away from the UFC, I got the urge to return. The UFC had filled up with a barrage of exceptional competitors, and I wanted to be among the mix. I wanted to climb over them and reacquire the title belt.

My first opponent upon my return was Georges St. Pierre, an all-around mixed martial arts fighter. I didn't take the fight lightly, but I didn't train as hard as I should have. I definitely didn't train the six hours that I do now.

I don't feel that Pierre outfought me; I feel I was out-conditioned. Nothing that Pierre did during the course of battle hurt me, but he did an excellent job getting ahead on the judges' scorecards by pinning me up against the cage and scoring takedowns. I was disappointed with the loss, but at the same time it showed me holes in my game that I needed to plug. It reminded me of just how important it is to constantly be learning and evolving.

I didn't expect to get a shot at the title anytime soon after my loss to Pierre, but when Pierre suffered an injury, I was called in to battle Hughes. Just as it was when I fought Hughes the first time, I knew there was no way I could lose. I trained hard every day, getting into peak cardiovascular condition. My game plan was to punish him with strikes, defend his takedowns, put him on his back, and smash him in the face just like I had the first time. Although this had been my game plan with Pierre, I had learned from that loss and trained for a five-round war.

In the first couple of rounds my game plan played out perfectly, and I got more confident with each second that passed. Toward the end of the second round, Hughes managed to put me on my back. As he came down with an elbow strike to my face, I slipped underneath his elbow, spun around his body, and took his back (p 192).

When you take an opponent's back, you have all sorts of offensive options and your opponent has next to none. It's a position from which you can end the fight at any moment. Some fighters like to get risky from the back and quickly execute a submission, but I like to take my time. Usually I'll soften my opponent up with strikes, bloody him a little, and then gradually slip in a submission such as a rear naked choke. But when I got Hughes's back, I didn't have the luxury of time. In addition to there only being a minute left in the round, I had also felt one of my ribs blow out when I made the transition to his back. If I couldn't lock in a submission before the minute was up, I would be in trouble at the beginning of the third.

Immediately I went for a reverse triangle choke. Hughes defended perfectly, so I went for an arm bar from the reverse triangle position. I put everything I had into it, but without first softening Hughes up with strikes, he remained strong and avoided the submission attempt.

Although I knew I was hurt when I took a seat in my

corner after the second round, I still thought I could win. In my mind, it was destiny. When you have a hardcore mind-set like that, you truly believe nothing can get in your way. On top of that, all the people in attendance had paid money to see the fight. If you're not willing to give a 110 percent, you shouldn't even be in the cage. Giving up never even crossed my mind.

I headed back out at the beginning of the third, but every move I made sent pain shooting through my side. I knew I had to baby my ribs, so when Hughes threw a left body hook, I curled my whole body in and tried to block the shot with my leg. Immediately Hughes recognized that I was injured. He capitalized on my weakness by shooting in and scoring a takedown, ending up in my half guard.

In the beginning of my jiu-jitsu career, the one thing I focused on more than anything was not letting my opponents pass my guard. It's something I spent a lot of time perfecting, and as a result no one had ever passed my guard in jiu-jitsu competition or a fight. I felt confident that I could prevent Hughes from transitioning to side control, but then he started dropping shots to my injured ribs. The pain was excruciating. I was using my left arm to prevent him from passing, but I was forced to draw that arm in to protect my ribs.

Immediately Hughes transitioned to side control and captured me in what I like to call the Beat Down Position (p. 239), and that's exactly what he began to do—beat me down. I still believed there was no way I could lose, so when the referee pulled Hughes off of me, I thought I had escaped. I like to think that if I had slipped out of his hold I could have reacquired control, but that's probably not how things would have played out. With my ribs busted up like they were, Hughes most likely would have claimed the mount and continued his assault.

It took some time for the loss to sink in. Several of my friends said that I should never have headed back out for the third round injured, but I would much rather get pounded than throw in the towel and get booed out of the arena. I blamed the loss on a freak accident in the coming days, but I now realize that's not what happened. I lost the fight due to improper conditioning. I was in excellent cardiovascular condition, but I wasn't in perfect physical condition. The reason I say this is because I hadn't focused on being the best athlete I could every day of the year. Six months out of the year I managed to stay in shape, but I wasn't staying in peak shape. Then for a fight I would suddenly do what I needed to be one of the top athletes in the world. It doesn't work that way. My rib broke not because I was unlucky, but rather because I hadn't stayed in flawless fighting shape year-round. If I had been doing five thousand sit-ups every day and eating healthy meals every time I sat down at the table, my rib would most likely have held fast.

To reach the highest levels of this sport you must be on a constant quest to better yourself as a person and a fighter. You should strive to be number one every day of your life, not just when you're actively fighting. You must keep an open mind and experiment with new strategies and techniques. The sport continues to evolve every day, and if you're not willing to learn from your losses and mistakes, you're going to get left behind. The fight with Hughes reminded me just how important all these factors are. If you keep these things in mind as you struggle up the ladder, you will find success. It might not come today or tomorrow, but it will come. With undying determination, you can reach the top of any mountain.

The Sport of Mixed Martial Arts

Mixed Martial Arts is one of the most intricate sports in the world. It involves techniques and strategies from Brazilian Jiu-Jitsu, Muay Thai kickboxing, boxing, wrestling, judo, jeet kune do, and virtually every other martial art ever developed. Pit two fighters from one of these martial arts together and the possibilities of what can happen in the ring are immense. Pit two fighters together who have picked and studied techniques and strategies from a number of these arts, and then blended those techniques into a highly individualistic fighting style, the possibilities of what can happen in the ring or cage are nearly endless. This is what makes the sport of MMA so profound and amazing. No matter how badly a fighter is getting beaten, there is always something that he can pull out of his arsenal to turn the tide and gain the upper hand.

Having limitless possibilities in a sport gives you greater leeway to create your own style. Mixed martial arts is regimented in that you must have prowess in striking, takedowns, and grappling, as well as the ability to seamlessly blend all three aspects of the game together, but it is far from militaristic because you have the freedom to choose which aspect of the game will be your bread and butter. Some say that certain styles are better than others to have as your base, but it really just boils down to the individual. Some people are naturally better strikers, while others are born to grapple. Some fighters rely upon physical attributes and conditioning to come out on top, while others depend upon technique. Over the years, MMA champions have hailed from all sides of the coliseum. Every fighter is different both physically and mentally, and if your desire is to become an MMA champion, you must discover what works best for you.

If you're already an accomplished grappler or kickboxer, you don't have to go searching for your base. It is important that you rely upon the techniques that have been ingrained into your DNA. I have seen many exceptional wrestlers enter MMA, feel inclined to turn it into a boxing match, and lose as a result. I have also seen many amazing kickboxers feel inclined to take their opponent down and wind up getting submitted. All the fighters from a specific martial arts background who have climbed to the top of the MMA mountain have done so by relying upon their primary discipline. Wrestlers rely upon takedowns and ground 'n' pound. Strikers rely upon punches and kicks and knees to knock their opponent out. Jiu-jitsu practitioners rely upon submissions.

UFC competitor Randy Couture is first and foremost a wrestler. He is constantly adding strikes into his game, but he does so in such a way that the new techniques make him a better wrestler. UFC competitor Mirko Crocop is primarily a striker, but he is constantly improving his sprawls and grappling techniques so he can return to a position from which he can strike. My base is in jiu-jitsu. I haven't added too many kicks into my style because I haven't found them to be very conducive to my primary art, but I'm constantly adding in new boxing techniques that set me up perfectly for a takedown. I don't always choose to take my opponent down—often I choose to bang it out on my feet—but I have set my style up in such a way that I can always revert back to my base in moments of trouble or if a fight isn't going my way.

Now, if you're entering the sport of MMA without a background in wrestling or kickboxing or jiu-jitsu, you're going to have to find what aspect you gravitate toward. In the beginning you should spend an equal amount of time on the mats as you do with the boxing gloves on, but once you have found your specialty, the discipline you gravitate toward and have the most fun with, hone in on it. If it happens to be jiu-jitsu, you still want to train striking and wrestling, but you want to head for your black belt in jiu-jitsu. If striking is your thing, you still want to wrestle and train submissions, but you want your black belt in striking. I realize that if I had all the striking, wrestling, and takedown ability I do now, but I had a purple belt in jiu-jitsu rather than a black belt, I would not have gone this far in the sport of MMA.

However, after spending some time developing your base it is important not to get tunnel vision. Continuing to incorporate moves from other styles is a must. For strikers, those additions will be learning how to sprawl and stop the takedown, as well as learning how to control your opponent on the ground so you can return to your feet. It is vice versa for a grappler. He will add strikes into his style to gain the ability to hurt his opponent on his feet and work far enough inside to where he can execute a takedown. Although it can sometimes be difficult learning the intricacies on how to best blend styles, this book will certainly help you with this task.

Training at 80 Percent

There is an answer for every technique your opponent can utilize in training and in the cage. Going all out at a 100 percent often hinders you from seeing that answer. Toning things down 20 or 25 percent keeps your mind clear, which allows you to react to what your opponent is doing. It makes you quicker because your body is relaxed, as well as prevents you from gassing out after executing three or four techniques. The same philosophy applies to most sports. If you watch a world-class sprinter in action, you'll see that although he is madly sprinting for the finish-line, his body and face are relaxed. You should still push yourself past your boundaries as often as you can, but when fighting you want to maintain a 75-80 percent exertion level.

Training for a Fight

Competing in MMA requires a lot more than just having a large arsenal of techniques. To be successful in the sport, you must do a vast amount of cross training, physical strength training, cardiovascular conditioning, and flexibility training. You must also have a solid nutrition plan. Although each of these requirements are crucial for surviving in the cage, the aim of this book is to show techniques and offer strategies. However, I wanted to touch base on a few of these topics and include a couple of circuit workouts that have worked for me over the years. There are dozens of books that focus specifically on these facets, and if your goal is to compete, I suggest seeking a few of them out.

Sports Specific Fight Gone Bad

Executing the "Sports Specific Fight Gone Bad" circuit a few times before an upcoming fight is an unbelievable way to get into shape both physically and mentally. The idea of the circuit is to simulate your upcoming fight. If your bout is scheduled for three, five-minute rounds, then your circuit will last three, five-minute rounds. Although each round will consist of the same drills, you will be doing a different drill each minute in the round. For example, if your bout has five minutes per round, you will be doing five separate drills, each lasting one minute. If your bout has ten minutes per round, you will be doing ten separate drills, each lasting one minute.

Deciding which drills to include in your rounds should be based upon your attributes and game plan, as well as your opponent's attributes and game plan. Generally what I like to do is make a list of ten things that I will most likely need in my upcoming fight. For example, if you're primarily a grappler and your opponent is an excellent striker, then you might include on your list "Striking to the Takedown," "Guard Passes," and "Mount Attacks." If you're primarily a striker and your opponent is an excellent grappler, you might want to include on the list "Defending against the Takedown," and "Mount Escapes." As you can see there are an endless number of drills you can include; the important part is choosing drills that will actually help you in your fight. They should all be sports specific.

Once you've got your list, you want to choose five drills (based upon five minutes per round) from that list on the day you plan to execute the "Sports Specific Fight Gone Bad" circuit. Then you need to gather up five training partners and assign a drill to each one of them. For instance, if you assigned "Mount Escapes" to Training Partner #1, his only job will be to remain mounted on top of you, and your only job will be to escape. If you've assigned "Defending against the Takedown" to Training Partner #2, his only job will be to get you to the ground, and your only job will be to prevent him from doing so. You're still sparring as hard as you normally would; the only difference is you're trying to accomplish a specific goal.

After assigning all of the drills, climb into the cage and begin with Training Partner #1. As he goes all out to accomplish his goal, you go all out to accomplish your goal. If your goal is to stay mounted and your opponent escapes, you want to briefly stop the action so you can reacquire the mount. You do this for one minute. The instant that minute is up, Training Partner #2 jumps in and you attempt to achieve your second task for one minute. As you move through your partners, you want your cornerman to constantly encourage you from the sidelines while everyone else surrounding the cage cheers for your opponent.

Once you've gone through all of your partners, you take a minute break. Because this is a simulated fight, you want to have guys standing by to dump water on your head and rub your shoulders. Basically, bring you back to life for the next round. There should also be someone standing off to the side with a timer, making sure your next partner is ready to go each minute.

The trick with running the "Sports Specific Fight Gone Bad" circuit is not getting discouraged. Each minute you will be facing a training partner who is fresh, so expect to pretty much get dominated at every turn. A million thoughts will undoubtedly be running through your head: I want water, I can't go any longer, why am I doing this, screw all of you guys on the side. As these thoughts attack you from all angles, it is important to remember that the goal of this circuit is not to defeat your partners, because such a goal will be impossible under the conditions. Each minute you face a new animal, while you get more and more fatigued. The goal of the circuit is to push yourself past your limits and develop mental and physical stamina.

SAMPLE "SPORTS SPECIFIC FIGHT GONE BAD CIRCUIT"

(1st Minute) Striking For The Takedown

Strike at your partner and consistently work for the takedown.

(2nd Minute) Pressing Opponent against the Cage

While pressing your opponent against the cage, throw strikes and go for takedowns. If your opponent escapes the position, reset.

(3rd Minute) Fighting from the Sprawl

Let your opponent secure your legs in the shot position, and then work your sprawl and escapes. The moment you escape, reset.

(4th Minute) Ground 'n' Pound

From your opponent's guard, use ground and pound techniques to set up a pass. The moment you pass your opponent's guard, reset.

(5th Minute) Side Control

Starting in the top side control position, work to strike your opponent, lock in submissions, and transition to the mount or back. Once you complete a transition, reset.

Fight Gone Bad (Cross-Fit)

While the "Sports Specific Fight Gone Bad" circuit will do wonders to prepare you for your upcoming war in the cage, it is still important to supplement that training with a purely strength and cardio-conditioning circuit. There are many different circuits that you can do, but the Fight Gone Bad Cross-Fit circuit has worked the best for me over the years.

Instead of doing a different drill for each minute in your rounds, you're going to do a different exercise. Since you will be pushing, pulling, punching, dodging, and slamming your opponent in the ring, these are the types of exercises you should include on your list.

You won't need five training partners for this circuit, but it helps to have two. The first training partner will lead you from station to station, as well as keep track of time and reps. Every rep you do at each station will count as a point. At the end of each round your training partner will add up all the points you earned, and that will be your goal to beat in your next round. You're second training partner's only job will be to motivate you. As you move from one round to the next, you will become more and more exhausted. Having someone giving constant encouragement helps more than you can imagine.

SAMPLE "FIGHT GONE BAD (CROSS-FIT) CIRCUIT"

(1st Minute) Medicine Ball Squats

Have your training partner grab a medicine ball and stand on the edge of something that is elevated five feet off the ground (if you have an elevated ring, this tends to work best), while you stand beneath him. As your opponent drops the ball in front of your face, catch the ball and squat down. The instant you reach the bottom of your squat, explode upward and throw the ball back up to your partner. Keep going until the minute is up. (If you don't have an elevated platform, bouncing the ball off an open wall will work fine.)

(2nd Minute) Upright Rows

Grab the forty-five-pound weight lifting bar. Making sure your knees are bent and your back is straight, heft the bar up to your chin and then bring it back down to your waist. Do this as many times as you can until the minute is expired.

(3rd Minute) Box Jumps

Move over to the two-foot box and jump up and down as many times as possible for one minute.

(4th Minute) Military Press

Return to the forty-five pound bar and hoist it up onto your chest while in the standing position. Once there, extend the bar upwards over your head and then bring it back down to your chest.

(5th Minute) Row Machine

Climb onto the row machine and do as many reps as you can for one minute straight. Since this is your last minute in the round, give everything you have. (At this station, I count each calorie burned as one point.)

(6th Minute) Break

Breathe deep and recover. Have one of your training partners bring you back to life by pouring cold water on the back of your neck and massaging your shoulders. At the forty-second mark, stand up and get ready for your next round.

The Holyfield Circuit

The Holyfield is a great circuit for developing muscle endurance, and like all circuits it is a test of heart. In order to get started, you'll need to find a grassy field to do your workout, and then put a marker forty yards from the starting line and another marker ten yards from the starting line. (Football fields tend to work best because the yardage is already measured out.) You'll also need two training partners, one to keep track of time and one to assist you with the exercises.

Instead of choosing one exercise to do each minute of your rounds, you have a set list of exercises that you will do back to back until the round is over. If you're in excellent shape you might run through the list a couple of times before the round is over, and if you're not in excellent shape you might only make it through the list once. The important part is not stopping until the round is over. After you take your one-minute break at the end of each round, you want to immediately get started on your next round. As with the Fight Gone Bad circuits, you want to do the same number of rounds scheduled for your upcoming fight.

HOLYFIELD CIRCUIT

1. Sprint forty yards and backpedal to the starting line.

2. Jump as high as you can ten times.

3. Have your partner grab your feet and hoist your legs off the ground. Crawl to the ten yard line on your hands, and then crawl backwards to the starting line. Turn sideways, crawl to the ten yard line on your hands, and then crawl back to the starting line.

4. Do ten pushups, exploding off the ground and clapping your hands between each one.

5. Climb to your feet and karioka (sideways running while crisscrossing your legs) to the forty yard line and back.

6. Skip to the forty yard line and back.

Sample Circuit

A circuit can be whatever you want it to be as long as it is relevant to your fight. Below I've created a hypothetical list to get your ideas flowing. At the top of the list, I've included ten exercises that will help with getting in shape for a fight, and on the day of your circuit you want to choose five exercises from that list to include in your rounds. Remember, the whole point of a circuit is to kill yourself. If you don't get utterly exhausted during the circuit, then you're probably not doing it right.

Sample Circuit List

1. MIXING STRIKES UP ON THE HEAVY-BAG
2. ISOLATING STRIKES ON THE HEAVY-BAG
3. FOCUS MITTS
4. THAI PADS
5. SPRAWLS
6. OPEN SHOTS
7. BUNGEE SHOTS
8. GROUND 'N' POUND
9. PLYOMETRICS
10. ROW MACHINE

Sample Circuit

1st Minute - Mixing punches, kicks, and knees up on the heavy-bag.
2nd Minute - Sprawls (as many as possible).
3rd Minute - Ground 'n' pound drills on the heavy-bag.
4th Minute - Bungee shots.
5th Minute - Row machine.

Sample Sprint Workout

5 X 100-yard sprints (walk back to starting line after each sprint)
5 X 50-yard sprints (walk back to starting line after each sprint)
5 X 25-yard sprints (walk back to starting line after each sprint)
5 X 10-yard sprints (walk back to starting line after each sprint)

Running and Sprints

In addition to doing circuits, it is also important that you get in your sprints and long-distance runs when training for a fight. Although sprints are usually not on the top of a fighter's "favorite thing to do" list, it is important to get your heart rate up and develop that explosive speed and power needed for battle. Usually I'll do my sprint work the day before I have a day off so my body can adequately recover. If I do them at the beginning of my training week, I'm usually sore for several days and it has a negative effect on my training.

Going for long-distance runs develops endurance, helps you set a pace for breathing, and synchronizes your body and mind. A long run once every second week will usually allow you to reap some good benefits, but it is important to always listen to your body. It is a fine line between pushing yourself too hard and not hard enough. If I'm going to push myself to exhaustion, I would much rather do it through sparring or conducting fight-simulated drills because they're directly correlated to what I'll be doing in the fight.

Part One
THE STAND-UP GAME

The stand-up game in MMA isn't just about striking. It's about being able to set up your takedowns off strikes. It's about how proficient you are at avoiding the takedown. It's about how well you can fight from the clinch, and how well you can battle while pressed up against the cage. There are so many elements to the stand-up game that at times it seems impossible to keep up, but if you desire to become a true mixed martial artist, that's exactly what you must do.

The bottom line is that every time you step into the cage you will have to use different techniques to reach your goal. If your goal is to keep the fight standing, you will not use the same techniques when fighting a powerful wrestler as you would when fighting a fellow striker. If you want the fight on the ground, you'll use different techniques when fighting a powerful striker than you would when fighting a fellow grappler. The only way to tailor your game plan for the array of opponents you can face is to become well versed in all aspects of the stand-up game.

To help you with this monumental task, I've organized the Stand-Up Game into sections. Each section covers a facet critical to the MMA fighter. Whether you are primarily a striker or a grappler, you will find numerous techniques in each section that will help you achieve your goal in nearly any scenario. However, it is important that you study and break down each technique laid out in the upcoming sections, even if they don't suit your style. You'll want to do this because in order to learn how to defend against a certain technique, you must first understand how it is executed.

Experimenting with all the techniques will also help you understand the core principles of how techniques need to be blended together to maximize their effectiveness. This book lays out my style, which might not fit you perfectly, but as long as you hold on to the core principles I offer while training and experimenting, it's only a matter of time until you discover what works best for you.

STANCE

The foundation of every fighter's stand-up game is his stance. It's good to find a stance that fits your style, but it must be conducive to both the striking and grappling aspects of the sport. If you can throw excellent strikes from your stance but have a difficult time dropping your level to shoot in or sprawl, you have a serious weakness. If your stance is well suited for shooting and sprawling but not for striking, you also have a serious weakness. It's fine to tailor your stance to make the most of your strengths, but you can't leave any holes as a result. In MMA, it is imperative that you cover all bases.

As you work to develop your stance, it is important to keep a few requirements in mind. The most important of these requirements is that you keep your hands up at all times. It doesn't matter if you grossly outclass your opponent in the striking department; the moment you drop your hands, you give your opponent a puncher's chance. To protect your face when throwing a punch, you want to keep your opposite hand up, tuck your chin, and shrug your shoulders slightly to guard your jaw.

Maintaining balance is also crucial. If your feet are spread too far apart or too close together, your opponent will be able to topple your base. And when your base gets toppled, you're pretty much a fish out of water. The general rule of thumb is to keep your feet spread roughly a shoulder's width apart. This holds true even as you move about the cage. If you want to move to the left, step with your left foot and then follow with your right. If you want to move to your right, step with your right foot and follow with your left. You never want to cross your feet or get too spread out.

However, due to the erratic nature of combat, you won't always be able to maintain a perfect stance. No matter what position you should be forced into, it is important to always be balanced because that balance is what allows you to attack and defend. If you only feel comfortable and have balance when in your traditional stance, every time you are pushed or knocked out of that stance, your entire offense and defense goes straight out the window. Acquiring balance and mobility doesn't always come easy, but it is worth your time and attention. A dangerous MMA fighter is one who can attack and defend from any position.

Key Concepts For Stance

✓ Keep your feet roughly a shoulder's width apart.
✓ Never cross your feet.
✓ Knees slightly bent.
✓ Hands up.
✓ Shoulders shrugged.
✓ Chin Tucked.

STANDARD STANCE

This is the stance that I will usually assume when striking with an opponent. It is important to notice that although my hips are angled away from my opponent, making it difficult for him to shoot in for a double-leg takedown, my shoulders are facing forward. This allows me to better defend against takedowns and throw quicker punches. While in this stance, I remain relaxed and balanced, throwing strikes whenever I see an opening. I am also prepared on a moment's notice to drop into a crouched stance to defend against a takedown or shoot in on my opponent. It is important to mention that even though I am laying out two distinct stances (standard and crouched), your level will most likely rise and fall regularly due to the erratic nature of battle. For this reason, it is important to learn how to maneuver and acquire balance no matter what position you end up in. For example, when slipping a punch you won't always have time to step to the side. Sometimes you'll only have time to move your head out of the way. If you can't find your balance in this new and sometimes awkward position, it will be very difficult to launch an effective counter-attack.

With my shoulders facing my opponent, I keep my lead foot pointing forward and my rear foot angled to my right. My hands are up to protect my face, my elbows are tucked to my sides to protect my ribs, and my knees are slightly bent.

CROUCHED STANCE

I'll assume a crouched stance when preparing to shoot in on my opponent for a takedown, defend against a takedown attempt by sprawling, or evade a strike such as a hook. Sometimes I will also drop into a crouched stance to trick my opponent into thinking that I'm going to shoot in for a takedown. When he sees my level go down, he will usually drop his level (and sometimes his hands) to sprawl. Instead of shooting in from the crouched stance, I'll immediately pop back up into the standard stance and unleash with more strikes, catching him off guard. You can even unload with strikes from the crouched stance. Although this might take some time to get used to, mastering striking from all levels is a great way to increase your versatility.

To drop your level all you have to do is relax your legs and let gravity bring you down. One common mistake people make is that they bend forward rather than crouch down. This will not only hinder your maneuverability, but it is also a good way to get your head kicked off. You want to maintain tight posture, but not so tight that it hinders your movement. Keeping your balance and utilizing proper form will allow you to explode in any direction or come right back up to the standard stance with ease.

I achieve the crouched stance by dropping my hips and squatting straight down. My legs are now bent at a forty-five degree angle, and my head is aligned over my lead knee. I keep my hands up by my face, my chin tucked, and my shoulders slightly shrugged to protect my jaw.

STRIKING

There are hundreds of strikes that you can utilize in MMA, but to cover them all would be veering away from a book on MMA. In the upcoming section I've only included the strikes that have worked for me time and again in competition. As you will notice, I didn't include any kicks. The reason for this is because I haven't found kicks to be conducive to my primary style, which is jiu-jitsu. This isn't to say that kicks are not suitable for MMA, because they are. I just prefer punches because they allow me to transition directly into a takedown, and a takedown is what allows me to unleash my jiu-jitsu. Unless you've been living in a box or have been blind your entire life and just got a new set of eyes, you'll probably have seen the upcoming strikes before. However, I cover them not in the context of boxing or kickboxing, but rather in the context of MMA. You will be using these strikes later in the book to help set up other techniques both while standing and on the ground, so it is important to master the dynamics of each one.

Key Concepts For Striking

✓ When you punch, keep your opposite hand up to protect your face from counter punches.
✓ Always remain relaxed.
✓ Keep your chin tucked.
✓ When you punch, the shoulder attached to your punching hand should come up and protect your chin.
✓ Make contact with the knuckles of your middle and index fingers.
✓ Don't let your punch hang out—speedy recovery is just as important as a speedy attack.
✓ Don't let yourself get too spread out when you punch.
✓ Don't telegraph your punches by loading up.
✓ Put punches together into combinations whenever possible.
✓ Vary the level of your punches to increase your effectiveness.
✓ Get your hips involved as much as possible.
✓ As a rule of thumb, you want to exhale upon impact.
✓ Clinch your fist upon impact.
✓ Strike when within range.
✓ Use angles and proper footwork to gauge distance.
✓ Use side-to-side movement to set up your attacks.

JAB

Due to the small gloves used in MMA competition, the jab can cause a lot more damage than it does in boxing. It generally doesn't have knockout power, but a stiff jab can certainly break your opponent's nose or open a cut. The jab is also an excellent tool to set up other techniques such as a right cross or a takedown. Putting a quick fist in your opponent's face temporarily blinds him, which helps you sneak your next technique past his guard. Although you can throw the jab directly from your stance, taking a small step forward is the best way to generate power behind the blow. If your goal is to bring the fight to the ground, taking the step will also make it easier to transition into a takedown. The jab is the most important punch in boxing, and this rings true in MMA as well. It's not a punch you want to overlook.

From the standard stance, I throw my left fist straight out. I make sure to keep my right elbow tucked to my body and my right hand up for protection. As my left fist reaches the end of its path, I rotate my fist over so that my palm is pointing down. You want to strike your target with the knuckles of your index and middle fingers. It is important to notice that I keep my feet spread a shoulder's width apart.

SPECIAL NOTE: There are two types of jabs I like to utilize; the power jab and the snap jab. With the power jab, I step my lead foot forward and power my strike in to cause the most damage. When executing the snap jab, I keep both feet grounded in my stance and simply snap my fist into my opponent's face.

CROSS

The right cross will probably be one of the most powerful punches in your arsenal, and it works wonderfully off the jab because of how the jab cocks your hips and shoulders. Just as with all strikes, you want to throw the cross with the intent of doing damage. A lot of competitors who get intimidated in a fight will shadow box five feet away from their foe. You're not going to win a fight this way, so step in and throw. A good target to aim for is your opponent's chin. The cross is the holy grail of punches—if you land it, your opponent will be in pain.

Rotating my hips in a counterclockwise direction, I throw my right hand straight out and come up onto the ball of my right foot. As my fist nears its target, I rotate my hand over so that my palm is pointing down. As with all punches, you want to clinch your fist tight as you make contact, as well as strike with your first two knuckles.

HOOK

You can land the hook with your fist perpendicular to the ground or horizontal. I prefer keeping my fist perpendicular because I feel it's more powerful and it seems to come naturally. In addition to possessing knockout power, the hook is also a very hard punch to block because it travels on a circular path rather than a linear one. And even if your opponent manages to put his arm up to block, your hook still has a chance of sneaking around his blockade due to the small gloves used in MMA competition. The other nice thing about the hook is that it sets you up perfectly to transition into a takedown. It is by far my favorite punch in MMA because of its power and versatility.

Snapping my hips in a clockwise direction, I throw my left fist on a circular path. It is important to notice that my arm is bent at a forty-five degree angle, and that my fist and elbow are traveling along the same plain. To protect my face, I keep my left shoulder shrugged and my right hand held high.

OVERHAND

In addition to being a great counter when slipping straight punches, the overhand is also a wonderful answer to some of the problems that can arise in the cage. If you get rocked with a punch, throwing an overhand is a good way to back your opponent up and get him off you. If your opponent is continuously chopping away at your legs with kicks, throwing an overhand is a good way to make him think twice about doing it again. The overhand is responsible for some of the most brutal knockouts in the sport, and if you work on developing your accuracy, timing, and sense of distance in training, the punch will usually yield good results in a fight.

Dropping my left shoulder and rotating my hips in a counterclockwise direction, I shift my weight onto my left leg, come up onto the ball of my right foot, and throw my right hand in an upward arc (the motion is similar to a swimmer's freestyle stroke). You want to keep your left hand up to protect your face and make contact with the knuckles of your index and middle fingers.

UPPERCUT

There are a couple of different ways to throw the uppercut. The first option is to drop down into a crouched stance to chamber your hips and hand, and then come up with the full authority of your weight. The second option is to simply throw the uppercut directly from the standard stance without dropping down. It doesn't pack as much power, but it is less telegraphic and will often catch your opponent off guard.

OPTION 1

I shift my weight back onto my right leg and chamber my hips and shoulders. To unleash the uppercut, I drive up off my right leg, rotate my hips in a counterclockwise direction, and throw my right fist upward at a ninety degree angle (this angle will obviously change depending upon the distance between my opponent and I.) As I drive my fist upward, I rotate my hand so that my palm is facing toward me. To protect my face, I keep my right shoulder shrugged and my left hand held up by my chin.

OPTION 2

Rotating my hips in a counterclockwise direction, I throw my right fist upward at a ninety degree angle. As I drive my fist upward, I rotate my hand so that my palm is facing toward me. To protect my face, I keep my right shoulder shrugged and my left hand held up by my chin.

STRIKING FOR THE TAKEDOWN

Meshing strikes with takedowns is a fundamental component of MMA that far too many fighters neglect. I especially notice this with wrestlers and jiu-jitsu practitioners. The striking aspect of the sport often makes them nervous, so they attempt to shoot blindly in from outside of the pocket to avoid getting hit. As a result, their opponent thwarts their takedown attempts time and again and they end up getting hit a whole bunch. With the majority of MMA fighters possessing excellent takedown defense, you've got to learn how to move into the pocket with strikes and then transition to a takedown in order to be successful. If you move into the pocket without strikes, your opponent will see the takedown coming. If you shoot in from five feet away, he will also see the takedown coming. In this day and age, stealth is a must.

Don't ever get locked into striking mode or takedown mode, because your intent can be read from a mile away. There is no need to have two modes—they should be blended together to keep your opponent guessing. Once you learn which takedowns work off which strikes, the number of combinations you can string together become limitless. It's good to find the "striking to takedown" combinations that work best for you, but you should be proficient at shooting in off every punch you throw because you never know which punch in a combo will create an opening to take your opponent down. Having a large arsenal of combos will also prevent you from becoming a predictable fighter. If you only shoot in after throwing a hook, it won't take long for your opponent to catch on. Every time you throw the hook, he will be prepared to block the takedown.

Another good way to avoid telegraphing your takedowns is to vary the number of strikes you throw before shooting in. Sometimes it will pay to shoot in off a single punch, and other times you'll want to shoot in after throwing three or four punches. But no matter what combo you utilize, it is important not to force the takedown. If you throw a combo and the opportunity to take your opponent down doesn't present itself, step out of the pocket and set up your next combination. This will sometimes get your opponent thinking that you want to trade punches, which can take some of his focus away from defending the takedown.

I cannot stress enough the importance of blending the striking aspect of the sport with the grappling aspect. If you separate the two during training, you will have to switch modes during a fight. In the split-second interim it takes you to switch modes, your opponent can prepare a defense or catch you off guard with a strike of his own. By endlessly practicing striking to takedown drills, you not only eliminate that mental shifting of gears, but you also condition your body to lash out with strikes one second and then change levels to shoot in for the takedown the next.

Single vs Double

In the upcoming section, I focus exclusively on the basic single- and double-leg takedowns. It is very important to learn how to set up both takedowns with strikes because it allows you to get the penetration needed for a successful takedown. I cover striking to the double-leg takedown first because that's what I'll go for when fighting an opponent in an orthodox stance. Shooting in off my left lead leg comes naturally to me, and with my opponent's left leg forward, I have the positioning needed to get my head to the outside of his body, wrap up both of his legs, cut the corner, and complete the double. If my opponent is standing in a southpaw stance, wrapping up both of his legs becomes very difficult because his rear leg is so far away from me. However, his lead leg is right there for the taking, so instead I will utilize the single-leg takedown. If you adopt this strategy, knowing which takedown to utilize comes easy. The difficult part is properly setting up your takedowns, so I recommend paying special attention to developing this aspect of your game.

Key Concepts For Striking To The Takedown

✓Blend striking and takedowns. Your takedowns should be executed with the same ease as your strikes.
✓Always keep your hands up as you drop your level to shoot in.
✓Only shoot in when in striking range. You must be able to physically touch your opponent at an arm's length in order

to execute a technical and effective takedown.

✓Don't get locked into striking mode or takedown mode. Blend both modes together.

✓Get creative with your set-ups, combinations, and takedown attacks. Your set-up will determine the success of your attack.

✓Learn the mechanics of each strike, and then learn which takedowns are most effective off that strike.

✓If you're fighting an opponent who has the same leg forward as you, work for the double-leg takedown. If your opponent has his opposite leg forward, work for a single-leg takedown.

STRIKING TO THE DOUBLE-LEG

DOUBLE-LEG TAKEDOWN

When you shoot in on an opponent, there are a few things you must always remember. The first is to keep your hands up. There are a lot of fighters who are masters at timing your shot and throwing a knee, kick, or uppercut, and the last thing you want is to get caught on the jaw as your weight is moving forward. For this reason, it is imperative that you don't reach for your opponent's legs until your head has made contact with his body. This might be hard for fighters who come from a wrestling background because they are used to swinging their arms out wide to scoop up their opponent's legs, but such a habit must be broken through hundreds of repetitions in the gym. Second, you must have proper balance when executing a shot. If you don't have good balance, you will not only fail at getting the takedown, but you will also be left in a vulnerable spot. Balance comes from simply maintaining good posture throughout the shot, and this is similar to keeping your hands up in that it can only come through time and repetitions.

Once you have shot deep and wrapped your arms around your opponent's legs, you want to step forward with your back leg, quickly cut the corner at an angle, and then finish the takedown. If you don't cut the corner, you are basically tackling your opponent to the ground. Tackles work, but they take a lot more energy to execute. Cutting the corner also allows you to land in side control and immediately get your offense going. If you forget to cut that corner and continue to drive your opponent backward, you might still get the takedown, but most of the time you will land in your opponent's guard, which means the bulk of your offense will most likely have to wait until you can pass your opponent's guard. Learning and drilling how to cut that corner is key, but sometimes things just don't go as planned. If your shot is extremely deep, sometimes your opponent will simply topple backward without you having to take a single step, landing you in his guard. Although this isn't the ideal situation, you still managed to get the fight to the ground.

I'm in a standard fighting stance, squared off with Paco in the pocket.

Dropping my level and assuming a crouched stance, I prepare to explode forward into a double-leg takedown.

I close the distance between Paco and I by exploding forward off my right foot. My hands remain up to protect my face from any strikes Paco might throw as I close the gap. It is important to notice the positioning of my left foot; I have placed it in-between Paco's legs, right on his centerline.

Driving my head to the left side of Paco's body, I wrap both arms around the back of his knees.

Continuing to drive into Paco using the momentum of my initial explosion, I step forward with my right foot. As I do this, I reestablish my base and realign my posture. It is important to notice that my right shoulder is directly above my right leg, and that I'm not hunched over.

Pushing off my right leg, I cut the corner by driving my weight to my left side. As I do this, I push my head into Paco's ribs and pull his legs to my right. To be more detailed, I lift Paco's left leg off the ground with my right arm and push into his right leg with my left arm.

The moment I come down onto the canvas, I start working to clear Paco's legs to prevent getting stuck in his guard. To avoid a scramble, I drive my weight into him.

Rotating in a clockwise direction, I clear Paco's legs, drop my weight down on him, and work to establish the side control position.

To secure the side control position, I reposition my right arm to the right side of Paco's body. This hinders him from turning into me and forcing a scramble. To learn your options from here, visit the side control attacks section.

STRIKING TO THE DOUBLE-LEG

HOOK TO DOUBLE-LEG TAKEDOWN

This is by far my favorite "striking to takedown" combination. The hook is a powerful strike that is hard to defend, but when you combine it with the double-leg takedown, it creates a nearly unstoppable technique. When I say "combine," I mean just that. It's not a left hook and then a double-leg takedown, but rather a "left-hook/double." The entire technique is executed in one motion.

The combination is highly effective anytime during a fight. Sometimes your hook will land but your opponent manages to block the takedown, and other times your opponent will block the hook but you will get the takedown. It is very difficult for your opponent to block both, especially when you become a master at combining them into one motion. It is a perfect example of how the striking and grappling aspects of the game can be blended together to discombobulate your opponent and do some serious damage. Once you get this technique down, practice throwing two left hooks in a row and then shooting in for the takedown. The first hook is your power shot, and the second hook is more to set you up for the takedown. If you're like me, you'll find that it works unbelievably well.

I'm in a standard fighting stance, squared off with Paco in the pocket.

I turn my hips and shoulders in a counter-clockwise direction, loading up for the left hook.

Turning my hips and shoulders in a clock-wise direction, I throw the hook. Notice how my left arm is parallel to the ground and my right arm is up to protect my face. As my hook whips around, I carry my momentum slightly forward so I can drop in for the double-leg takedown.

Dropping my level, I explode off my right leg and step my left foot between Paco's legs. Notice how I keep my right hand up to protect my face from any strikes Paco may throw as I close the distance between us.

As I enter for the double, I wrap both arms around the back of Paco's knees.

Using the momentum I generated off my initial explosion, I step forward with my right foot and continue to drive my weight into Paco. As I do this, I reestablish a sturdy base and realign my posture. This will allow me to cut the corner and take Paco down.

I step my left leg to the outside of Paco's right leg, and then push off my right leg and drive my weight to my left. As I do this, I also drive my head into Paco's ribs and pull his legs out to my right.

As I take Paco down, I clear his legs to avoid getting stuck in his guard. From here I will work to establish side control.

HOOK TO FAKE SHOT TO OVERHAND

The better you get at setting up your shots with strikes, the more success you will have taking your opponent to the ground. However, if you are up against an intelligent fighter, he will constantly read your movements much like a good poker player reads his opponent's face. He will search for signs that tell him when you are about to shoot in. He will analyze your game to search for patterns. If you always set your shot up off a left hook, he will discover this and be better prepared to defend against your shot the next time you throw a hook. However, making an opponent think he has figured out your patterns can come to your aid as long as you have the versatility to switch things up. If it is embedded in your opponent's mind that you will follow every hook with a takedown, a good option is to throw the hook and fake the shot. Your opponent will most likely drop his hands to defend the takedown, and that's when you come over the top with the overhand right. In order to be successful with this technique, you must be prepared to throw the overhand immediately off the hook. You still want to sell the shot by dropping your level, but it doesn't take much if your opponent is already expecting the double-leg to follow the hook.

I'm in a standard fighting stance, squared off with Troy in the pocket.

To load up for the left hook, I lean forward and turn my shoulders and hips in a counterclockwise direction.

As I throw the left hook, I drop my elevation as though I'm going to follow with a double-leg takedown. Troy drops his hands to defend the takedown.

The instant Troy drops his hands to stuff my shot, I come over the top with an overhand right, landing to his chin.

JAB TO DOUBLE-LEG TAKEDOWN

The jab-to-double-leg takedown doesn't flow nearly as well as the hook-to-double. The reason for this is because the dynamics of the hook allows you to immediately drop your elevation for the shot. The hook also doesn't knock your opponent backward, which means he remains within takedown range. However, the jab-to-double is a good technique to have in your arsenal because it increases your options. It's always good to change things up. When executing this technique, you can throw the jab with bad intentions in order to faze your opponent for the shot or you can simply throw it as a fake. If your intention is to land the jab, then you will have to wait until the jab makes contact before dropping your level for the shot. Trying to do both at the same will most likely make both techniques sloppy. However, it is entirely possible to throw a fake jab that has little power and drop your elevation to shoot in at the same time. This comes in especially handy after you've nailed your opponent repeatedly with jabs and he has become accustomed to reacting in such a way that opens him up for a takedown.

I'm in a standard fighting stance, squared off with Paco in the pocket.

I throw a straight left jab at Paco's chin. Notice how I keep my chin tucked and my right hand up to protect my face.

As I pull my jab hand back, I reset my base and drop into a crouched stance. Immediately I close the distance between us by exploding forward off my right foot and stepping my left foot between Paco's legs, right on his centerline.

I wrap both arms around the back of Paco's knees. From here I will finish with the standard double-leg takedown (p. 30).

CROSS TO DOUBLE-LEG TAKEDOWN

I always prefer to shoot in off a left-handed strike because it sets up my hips, base, and balance in such a way that I can flow directly into the takedown. Executing a takedown off a right-handed strike such as the cross is a little more difficult because it disrupts your wrestling base, which is mandatory for a healthy shot. You can still shoot in off the cross, but you must reset your base before you do so. There are two ways to do this. The first is to throw the cross, pull your hand back into your stance, reset your hips, and then drop into a crouched stance and take your shot. The second way, which I show here, is to throw the cross and then step forward with your right foot. This allows you to reset your hips and assume the wrestling posture needed for the takedown. I've found that this way is more explosive and direct, but it can change the way you shoot in. If you take a long step forward, you will be in a southpaw stance. A lot of fighters who come from a wrestling background actually prefer this because they are accustomed to exploding forward off their right leg when it's in front, but I like exploding forward off my right leg when it's back. In order not to steer too far from the familiar, I will just take a small step with my right foot to cover some distance and realign my base. As long as I haven't moved into a southpaw stance, I can still shoot in as I always do. It is important to learn both methods because you never know how your opponent will react to your assault. If you knock your opponent backward with the cross, you might need to take a long step and shoot in from a southpaw stance in order to get the takedown. The more techniques you have tucked away in your arsenal, the better chance you'll have at achieving your goal.

I'm in a standard fighting stance, squared off with Paco in the pocket.

Whipping my hips in a counterclockwise direction, I throw a straight right cross to Paco's chin.

Rather than resetting my base off the cross, I take a small step forward with my right foot. This small step is essential because it not only allows me to continue with my forward momentum, but it also allows me to reset my base and penetrate with a balanced shot.

The instant my right foot hits the ground, I blast off my right leg and step my left foot between Paco's legs. As I do this, I wrap both arms around the back of his knees. From here I will complete the double-leg takedown (p. 30).

FOUR PUNCH COMBO TO DOUBLE-LEG TAKEDOWN

This is a combination I learned from watching Mike Tyson fights, and it's a thing of beauty. The jab gets you to the inside, which sets you up to throw the hook to your opponent's body. The moment you land the hook, your opponent will most likely fold sideways under the power of the blow, which in turn sets you up nicely for the uppercut. The uppercut rocks your opponent's head back, creating an opening to land a left hook to his face. And as you have already learned, the left hook allows you to transition right into the double-leg takedown. There are countless different four-punch combinations that you can string together, but this is one of my favorites.

I'm in a standard fighting stance, squared off with Troy in the pocket.

I fire a straight left jab at Troy's chin. As my fist nears its target, I rotate my fist so that my palm is facing down. Ideally, you want to land flush with your first two knuckles.

As I draw my left hand back, I rotate my shoulders and hips in a counterclockwise direction. This allows me to throw a powerful right hook to Troy's body. It is important to notice that I have employed my hips in the punch by pivoting on the ball of my right foot.

Troy reacts to the body shot by dropping his elbow and coiling his body to his left, giving me an opening to land a right uppercut.

Having rotated my body in a counterclockwise direction to land the body shot, my arm and body are in perfect position to deliver an uppercut. I come straight up the middle, crashing my fist into Troy's chin.

The uppercut rocks Troy's head up and back, leaving his body vulnerable to a takedown. I make use of the opening by dropping my level, rotating my hips in a clockwise direction, and throwing a left hook to his body. This resets my hips and allows me to immediately shoot in for the double-leg.

Exploding off my right leg, I step forward with my left foot and wrap my arms around the back of Troy's knees. From here I will finish with a standard double-leg takedown (p. 30).

FAILED SHOT TO HOOK

When you shoot in for a takedown and your opponent stuffs your shot, you have a couple of different options. You can use all of your energy at one time and try to push through and complete the takedown. If you are a really good wrestler who is deathly afraid of your opponent's stand-up skills, perhaps you can manage it. Where there is a will there is a way. But in order to be a true mixed martial arts fighter you must be confident in all areas. You have to be able to mix things up. When you shoot in and your opponent blocks your shot, a good option is to pull out and then unload with punches. Because your opponent just assumed a defensive posture to counter your takedown, there is a good chance that you will catch him with his hands down. The moment he lifts his hands to defend your punches, you have another opportunity to shoot in and take him down. Even if you're a grappler who is fighting the best striker in the world, you can't be afraid to climb into the trenches and strike. The better you get at blending punches with your takedowns, the more dangerous you become.

I'm in a standard fighting stance, squared off with Reagan in the pocket.

I throw a left jab at Reagan's chin.

As I bring my left arm back into my stance, I rotate my hips in a counterclockwise direction and throw a straight right cross.

As I pull my right arm back into my stance, I rotate my hips in a clockwise direction. This allows me to throw the left hook, drop my elevation, and shoot in for a double-leg takedown all at the same time.

Reagan manages to get his arms underneath me. He steps back and stuffs my shot.

Rather than give up and disengage, I continue forward, rotating my hips and shoulders in a counterclockwise direction to load up for a powerful left hook.

Not expecting the immediate counter, Reagan gets plastered in the face.

SHOOTING TO CAGE TO TAKEDOWN

If your opponent stuffs your shot with a perfect sprawl and you know he's got you beat, working back to your feet is probably your best option. However, if your opponent sprawls and you feel that you might still be able to get the takedown, the cage can sometimes be your best weapon. Instead of working back to your feet, continue to drive forward until your opponent hits the cage. Once he is backed up against the chain link, he can no longer sprawl. This will sometimes allow you to get under his hips, pick him up, and slam him to the canvas.

I'm squared off with Albert in the pocket, ready to unleash my attack.

I turn my shoulders and hips in a counterclockwise direction to load up for the left hook.

Leaning forward, I throw a left hook to Albert's face.

As my left hook swings toward its target, I drop my level and shoot in for a double-leg takedown.

Albert manages to block my shot by dropping his hips low and sprawling his legs back.

Rather than give up on the shot and work back to my feet, I drop to my knees and continue to drive forward.

With Albert nearing the cage, I bring my left foot forward and post it on the mat.

Pushing off my posted left leg, I drive Albert into the cage. No longer able to sprawl, his hips are forced upward. This takes his weight off my back and allows me to climb to my feet.

Pinning Albert up against the fence, I wrap both arms around the back of his knees. Because of my positioning, I decide to pick Albert up, turn him away from the fence, and slam him. To learn your other options from here, visit the 'fighting against the cage' section.

Lifting Albert off the mat, I pivot in a clockwise direction so I have room to slam him to the mat.

Rotating my shoulders in a clockwise direction, I pull Albert's legs to my right, drive all my weight downward, and slam him to the mat. It is very important that you slam your opponent down using the shoulder you picked him up with. Because I picked him up on my left shoulder, I use my left shoulder to force him down.

DeSouza Special

You never want your head trapped underneath your opponent's armpit because it allows him to work for either a wrestler's front headlock or a guillotine choke. The most common way to end up in this position is when you shoot in with bad posture and expose your neck. You can also find yourself in this tight spot when your opponent pulls your head down from the clinch. Regardless of how it happens, it's not a position you want to hang out in. When I find myself with my head trapped underneath my opponent's armpit, I'll utilize the DeSouza Special, which I learned from Tony DeSouza, a world-class wrestler/jiu-jitsu player and friend. It's an excellent move because not only does it free your head, but it also gives you your opponent's back.

Having wrapped up my head, Albert is in a position to work for either a wrestler's front headlock or a guillotine choke. If he secures either hold, I will be in serious trouble, so I must immediately make my escape.

As Albert drops his hips and sprawls his legs back, he works to capture me in a front headlock.

Wasting no time, I come up onto my feet and swing my right arm all the way around Albert's back.

Hooking my right arm around Albert's right side, I maneuver my body in a counterclockwise direction so that I'm perpendicular to his body.

I press my head into Albert and drive forward off my legs. This topples his base and he crumbles to the mat.

As Albert collapses to his side, I secure his back by wrapping both arms around his body.

DEFENDING THE GUILLOTINE

If you shoot in with bad posture, it is quite possible that your opponent will sprawl, wrap an arm around your head, pull you up to the standing position, and attempt to finish you with a guillotine choke. You can also end up in this compromising position when your opponent pulls your head down while in the clinch. If you find yourself caught in a front headlock, you don't want to panic and pull away because it will usually allow your opponent to better synch in the choke. Instead, you want to utilize one of two options. If your opponent doesn't have the choke sunk tight, you can trip him or drive him back into the fence, which allows you to work for a double-leg takedown. If your opponent does have a tight lock on your neck, it's best to defend against the choke. In order to do this, you use one hand to create separation between your opponent's arm and your throat. At the same time, you throw your opposite arm up over his shoulder, as well as block him from driving his hips forward by digging your knee into his hips. These last two actions create separation between you and your opponent and hinder his ability to arch his back, which he must do in order to lock the choke tight. Once you achieve this defensive posture, it would be very foolish of your opponent to spend several minutes trying to lock in the submission. Not only would it waste precious energy, but it would also send a rush of blood to his arms, hurting his strikes and grappling later in the fight. Most opponents will simply let go and try something else. The only thing you really need to look out for when caught in the guillotine in the standing position is your opponent pulling you down into his guard. To learn how to escape when your opponent does this, visit the top guard section.

Having wrapped up my head, Butch is attempting to finish me with a guillotine choke.

Grabbing Butch's left wrist with my right hand, I pull his arm down to relieve pressure from my neck.

To relieve more pressure from the choke, I throw my left arm over Butch's right shoulder.

I lift my left leg and hook it around the inside of Butch's right leg. This blocks his hips and prevents him from being able to apply any real pressure with the choke.

Breaking Butch's grip with my right hand, I pry his arm away from my neck. Then I place my left foot on the mat and begin to back out and disengage.

As I back away, I keep my left hand up and continue to hold onto Butch's left hand. This prevents him from being able to punch me as I create separation between us.

Backing all the way out, I assume my standard fighting stance.

SHOOTING INTO GUARD

When you get stuck underneath your opponent in the sprawl position, your primary goal should be to get back to your feet. A secondary option is to sit down and trap your opponent between your legs in the guard position. This will put you on your back, which as you will learn in an upcoming section can be a very compromising position, so there should be some serious benefits if you choose this option. Perhaps you are taking serious abuse while trapped underneath your opponent. Perhaps your opponent is excellent at defending against takedowns but has no ground game whatsoever, and you feel confident that you can finish him from your back or sweep him over and claim the top position. It all depends upon the situation, but pulling guard simply because you want the fight on the ground is not good reasoning. If you really want the fight on the ground, a better approach would be to return to your feet and then utilize one of the techniques laid out in this book to bring the fight down and obtain the top position. Shooting into guard should generally be a last-ditch effort when all else fails.

Paco manages to block my shot by catching me with his left arm and sprawling his left leg back.

Although the double-leg takedown is out of reach, I still want to bring the fight to the ground, so I decide to shoot into guard. Posting on my left foot and right hand, I begin to slide my right leg in front of my body.

With my right leg now in front of me, I fall down onto my right hip and hook my left foot over Paco's right leg.

To capture Paco in my closed guard, I wrap my legs around his body and lock my feet together. To prevent him from posturing up, I wrap my arms around his head.

SINGLE-LEG TAKEDOWN

If you're in a standard stance fighting an opponent in a southpaw stance (right leg forward), it is very difficult to shoot in deep enough to execute a double-leg takedown because his hips are reversed. If you come from a wrestling background and are used to shooting in from a southpaw stance, the dilemma is easily remedied by throwing a strike, stepping forward into a southpaw stance, and then shooting for the double, but not everyone is accustomed to this. Instead of switching my stance, I tend to go for a single-leg takedown when fighting a southpaw. The only time I will go for a double in such a situation is when my opponent throws a left cross and I slip it. This changes the game because his hips are now centered and he will most likely be off balance, making that deep shot easier to manage. But the majority of the time you should be thinking about the single (if you're a southpaw fighter, then you'll want to focus on the single when fighting an opponent in an orthodox stance). The single is set up the same as the double; the only thing that changes is your entry into the takedown. Instead of stepping in-between your opponent's legs, you will step to the outside of his lead leg. You will also place your head to the inside of your opponent's body rather than the outside.

I'm in a standard fighting stance, squared off with Paco in the pocket.

I drop my level and step my left foot to the outside of Paco's lead leg.

Pushing off my right foot, I drive into Paco, place my head in the center of his chest, wrap my arms around his right leg, and grip my hands together.

Bending my legs slightly, I sit my base back, pinch my elbows together, and pull Paco's right leg up to my chest.

Keeping my left foot planted behind Paco's right leg, I drive my head into him. Notice how I am pinching his leg between my arms, chest, and left leg to keep it tightly secured.

Continuing to drive my head into Paco, I rotate in a counterclockwise direction and trip him backwards over my left leg.

I finish the takedown by climbing up to my knees and securing the top position.

CROSS TO HOOK TO SINGLE-LEG TAKEDOWN

Shooting in for a single-leg takedown off the left hook works just as well as shooting in for the double-leg takedown off the left hook. Your form will be the same in that you want to drop your level and begin your shot as you send the hook toward the side of your opponent's face. The only difference with this technique is that as you shoot forward you want to move your head toward the inside of your opponent's body and your lead leg toward the outside of his lead leg.

I'm in a standard fighting stance, squared off with Paco in the pocket.

I throw a right cross at Paco's face.

As I bring my right hand back, I rotate my shoulders and hips in a clockwise direction to load up for the hook.

Still whipping my hips and shoulders in a clockwise direction, I throw the hook. As my fist whips around, I allow my momentum to carry me slightly forward so I can drop in for the single-leg takedown.

Stepping forward with my right leg, I reach around the outside of Paco's right leg with my left arm and around the inside of his right leg with my right arm. To secure his leg, I clasp both hands together.

Stepping my left foot to the outside of Paco's right leg, I draw his leg up to my chest with my arms. From here I will continue with the standard single-leg takedown (p. 45).

OVERHAND TO SINGLE-LEG TAKEDOWN

The overhand right is another great punch that sets you up for a single-leg takedown against a southpaw. Throwing the overhand drops your elevation, but instead of coming back up and resetting your base, you want to use the momentum generated by the overhand to continue forward into the takedown. However, in order to be successful with the single-leg, you must get your head to the inside of your opponent's body.

I'm in a standard fighting stance, squared off with Paco in the pocket.

I turn my hips in a counterclockwise direction, come up onto the ball of my right foot, pull my left shoulder down, and cast my right hand out in an upward arc. Notice how my back leg is straight and my front leg is bent into the punch.

Instead of bringing my right hand all the way back into my stance, I reset my hips by taking a small step forward with my right foot. As I do this, I maneuver my head to the inside of Paco's body and wrap my left hand around the back of his right leg.

As my right foot comes down, I wrap both hands around Paco's right leg and pull it up to my chest.

I step my left foot behind Paco's right leg. From here I will complete the single-leg takedown and secure the top position (p. 45).

FAKE SINGLE TO OVERHAND

I see countless fighters get stuck in either striking mode or takedown mode. This not only limits their options, but it also makes them predictable. You must always keep your opponent guessing. When you scoop up your opponent's lead leg, it can sometimes be difficult to secure the takedown, especially if your opponent has good single-leg defense. Continuing to work for the takedown will sometimes pay off, and other times it will accomplish little more than burning a lot of energy. If you feel like you're wasting your time, a good option is to let go of the single-leg and throw an overhand right. A lot of the time your opponent will be so focused on hopping on one leg and defending the single-leg, he won't see the overhand coming. If you land the strike but don't knock your opponent out, you can swoop right back in and continue to work for the takedown. Once you land this move in a fight, the next time you secure your opponent's lead leg, you can guarantee he will be watching out for the overhand, which will take a portion of his focus away from defending the takedown.

Having shot in and secured Albert's right leg, I am working for the single-leg takedown.

Instead of fighting for the single-leg takedown, I remove my right hand from behind Albert's leg and prepare to throw an overhand.

Keeping Albert off balance, I land a right punch to his chin.

COUNTERATTACKS

Although it's important to always be offensive in a fight, at some point your opponent will throw an attack of his own. Falling victim to the attack is the worst possible scenario because it causes you damage and increases your opponent's confidence. Blocking the attack is better than getting hit, but it does little to sway your opponent from immediately launching another attack. The best possible scenario is to make your opponent's attack miss, and then launch an attack of your own while your opponent is still trying to recover from his failed attack. Not only does this eliminate any damage you might have suffered, but it also causes your opponent some pain. If you manage to inflict damage every time your opponent comes at you with an attack, his confidence will quickly shrivel and he will instinctively fall into defensive mode. This allows you to gain some serious offensive momentum. However, becoming a good counter-fighter does not come easy. It requires a keen sense of distance and impeccable timing, both of which must be earned through hours of drills and sparring in training.

Countering Strikes with Strikes

If you're primarily a striker and want to keep a fight standing, countering your opponent's strikes with strikes of your own is a good option. Deciding what counter strike to throw depends largely upon what strike your opponent threw and how you evaded it. When your opponent throws a straight jab down the center, you want to slip the punch by moving your head to the side. This gives you a couple of options. You could throw a jab of your own as you reposition your head, using the momentum of the slip to derive power for your punch. I personally like this option because you're making contact with your opponent's face as his punch sails by your ear. Another option is to slip the punch and then follow with a right hook, uppercut, or overhand. With this technique, your hips get coiled from the slip, and then you uncoil them to derive power for the punch. It's slightly slower than slipping and firing at the same time, but it packs a good deal of power. You're taking full advantage of your opponent's compromised positioning.

The same options are available when you slip the cross. You can immediately throw a right overhand, using the momentum of the slip to derive power for the punch, or you can coil your hips by slipping the cross, and then uncoil them to generate power for a lead hand strike such as a hook to the body or head.

If your opponent throws a looping punch such as a hook, things change a little. Because looping punches have to travel farther to reach their target than straight punches, a straight jab or cross is a great counter. The idea is to land your straight punch while your opponent's looping punch is still traveling on its circular path. Your other option is to slip the hook, which cocks your hips just like it does when you slip either the jab or cross. As your opponent's punch sails over your head, it throws him off balance and leaves one whole side of his body exposed. This creates an opening to land a hook to his body or head.

Learning how to counter strikes with strikes isn't just important for those who want to keep a fight standing. Even if you're a die-hard grappler, you will benefit from experimenting in this arena. Not only will it increase your chances of ending a fight with a knockout, but it will also increase your chances of executing a successful takedown. It's pretty much a win-win situation.

To develop the timing and sense of distance needed to properly counter strikes, have your training partner slip on a pair of focus mitts and throw punches at you. Avoid the punches by slipping from side to side, and then launch your counter-attacks at the mitts. Incorporate the countering techniques I show in the upcoming section into your shadow boxing and heavy bag training. And when sparring, constantly think about how you will deal with your opponent's strikes. Even when you're on the war path, you want to constantly be thinking about counter-fighting strategy.

Countering Strikes with a Takedown

Taking an opponent down in MMA competition is not always the easiest thing to accomplish, especially when going up against an opponent who is excellent at sprawling. If you shoot blindly in on an opponent who is standing in a proper stance just waiting for you to try and take him down, the chances are you're not going to achieve your desired outcome. Setting up your takedowns will dramatically improve your success rate. As I demonstrated in the last section, one way to do this is to unleash a combination of strikes at your opponent and then quickly transition into a takedown. Another way is to slip or duck one of your opponent's strikes and then quickly transition into a takedown. Any time your opponent throws a strike with conviction and you evade it, he will be vulnerable to a takedown for a brief moment.

A good way to develop the timing and skill needed to shoot in off an opponent's strike is to practice a drill I call "Striker vs. Grappler." To start off, your training partner will play the roll of striker and you will play the roll of grappler. His only goal is to land strikes and defend against the takedown, and your only goal is to avoid his strikes and get the takedown. In the beginning you should start very, very slow. You might even want your training partner to call out which strike he is going to throw until you are familiar with what they look like and how to evade them. Once you are comfortable with slipping the hook, jab, and cross at drilling speed, pick up the pace and turn it into a sparring drill. This will prime your reactions, as well as get you accustomed to slipping a strike in such a way that you have the proper base and balance for executing a shot. If you do not have that base and balance when you slip a strike, you do not want to execute the shot. Just reset and try to catch your training partner on his next strike. To prevent you from getting in the habit of running away from your partner's strikes, remain within striking distance for the duration of the drill.

I can't stress enough the important of this drill and others like it. To become a good MMA fighter, you not only need to understand the core principles of each discipline involved in the sport, such as kickboxing, wrestling, and jiu-jitsu, but you must also understand how to seamlessly blend those principals together so they work in conjuncture with one another. Every time you slip a jab or cross or hook there will be a select number of takedowns at your disposal due to the positioning of your body and your opponent's body, and drills such as "Striker vs. Grappler" allows you to learn those options. This is what the sport of MMA is all about. It is not about how good you are in wrestling or striking or jiu-jitsu—it is about how efficiently you can blend the basic principles from each of the main disciplines into a fighting style that makes your options infinite.

Key Concepts for Counterattacks

✓To effectively counter an opponent's attack, you must evade his attack and launch an attack of your own at the same time.
✓When avoiding an opponent's attack, only move as far as necessary.
✓As you slip from side-to-side to evade punches, maintain a solid base and keep your hands up.
✓When countering, base your attack on available openings.
✓A master counter fighter uses his defense as his offense.

SLIPPING LEFT JAB

The jab is by far the easiest punch to slip due to its angle of attack. Since it comes straight at you, all you have to do is slip your head to the side to avoid it. However, the jab only has a short distance to travel to reach your face and it is the quickest of all punches, so you must develop your reaction speed and sense of distance through thousands of repetitions in training. It is important to stay balanced while slipping, and it helps not to overdramatize your movement. You don't have to shift your head two feet to one side or the other; you only have to move it far enough to evade the punch. When done correctly, the nice part about slipping the jab is that it sets you up perfectly for the double-leg takedown, as well as a number of strikes.

I'm squared off with Albert in the pocket.

Albert throws a left jab at my face. As the punch comes toward me, I drop my right shoulder and maneuver my head to my right, allowing his fist to slip past my head. Notice how I keep both hands up and maintain a solid base.

Having successfully slipped Albert's jab, I return to my standard fighting stance.

COUNTER JAB WITH JAB

When possible, you want to avoid backing up and running away from an attack. As long as you possess the skills to make your opponent miss, it is much better to stand your ground or step forward because it will put you in range to counter with a takedown or strike of your own. However, in order to be successful with such a counter you must launch your attack before your opponent has a chance to recover from his missed attack. With this technique, you want to land your jab at the same moment your opponent was supposed to land his.

I'm squared off with Albert in the pocket.

As Albert throws a left jab at my face, I slip his punch by dropping my right shoulder and maneuvering my head to my right. At the same time, I begin thrusting a left counter jab at Albert's chin.

As Albert's punch goes sailing by my head, I land a firm jab to his chin.

COUNTERING THE JAB

COUNTERING JAB TO DOUBLE-LEG TAKEDOWN

Slipping the jab sets you up perfectly for a double-leg takedown, but the jab can sometimes be a difficult punch to slip. Because your opponent is striking with his lead hand, the jab comes at you a whole lot faster than the cross. Timing is imperative, and that comes from practice. When drilling in the academy there are a couple of different scenarios you should focus on. The first is when your opponent throws a long jab from outside the pocket. In order to get the take-down, you're going to have to slip the jab and step forward at the same time to cover the distance. If he throws from within the pocket, you should practice shooting for the takedown right off the slip. The nice thing about slipping either type of jab is that it places your head to the outside of your opponent's body, which means he doesn't have many op-'tions to counter with other strikes. He can't land his right hand and he can't land his right kick. However, anytime you go for a double-leg takedown you become susceptible to a guillotine choke because your head is essentially slipping underneath your opponent's arm. If you employ proper form and maintain good posture, you won't have to worry about the choke.

I'm in a standard fighting stance, squared off with Paco in the pocket.

Paco throws a left jab at my face. I slip his punch, drop my level slightly, and shift the majority of my weight onto my right leg.

Pushing off my right leg, I explode forward and wrap both arms around the outside of Paco's legs.

I step my right foot forward.

I step my left foot forward, and then immediately cut the corner by pushing off my right leg and driving to my left side. As I do this, I pull both of Paco's legs to my right.

I continue to cut the corner and follow Paco to the ground.

I follow Paco all the way to the ground and establish the top position.

SLIPPING THE CROSS

Although the cross is much harder to slip than the jab, you'll want to spend some time learning this technique because the cross is one strike you definitely want to avoid. The hard part for many is becoming accustomed to moving toward the punch as they slip it. It might seem unnatural at first, but it puts you in range to launch a counter-attack, which could be tying your opponent up with a body-lock and taking him down, throwing an overhand right, or striking to the body. When practicing the slip, it helps to look at your form in the mirror. Your body mechanics should look similar to when you throw a right cross, except with the slip you don't extend your right arm.

I'm squared off with Albert in the pocket.

As Albert throws a right cross at my face, I slip his punch by rotating my hips and shoulders in a counter-clockwise direction and leaning slightly to my left.

Having slipped Albert's cross, I return to my standard fighting stance.

SLIP RIGHT CROSS TO OVERHAND/HOOK COUNTER

When you slip an opponent's cross, the dynamics of the slip allows you to simultaneously throw an overhand right. If you choose this option, the momentum of your punch will pull your rear leg forward much like a baseball pitcher's rear leg comes forward after he throws the ball. This not only allows you to take a quick step forward and close the distance between you and your opponent, but it also loads up your hips to throw a left hook. It's an effective combination because as your opponent falls backward from the overhand, you step forward and catch him in the side of the jaw.

I'm squared off with Albert in the pocket.

Albert throws a right cross at my face. As his fist comes at me, I slip his punch by rotating my hips and shoulders in a counterclockwise direction. Using the momentum of the slip, I throw an overhand right.

As Albert's fist sails by the side of my face, I come around with an overhand right, nailing him square in the jaw.

I follow through with the overhand.

Allowing the momentum of my punch to carry my hips forward, I take a small step with my right foot. This locks and loads my hips to deliver a left hook.

I whip my hips in clockwise direction as I prepare to throw the hook.

Still rotating my hips in a clockwise direction, I smash a left hook into the side of Albert's already bludgeoned face.

SLIP CROSS TO 3 PUNCH COMBO

When you slip a right cross, the right side of your opponent's body becomes exposed, making it a good time to hammer a hook into his ribs. The body shot creates an opening for an uppercut, and the uppercut rocks your opponent's head back, making him vulnerable to a right cross. If you land all three shots flush, there is a good chance your opponent will go down.

I'm squared off with Albert in the pocket.

Albert throws a right cross at my face, and I slip his punch by rotating my hips and shoulders in a counterclockwise direction and leaning slightly to my left. Notice how slipping the cross loads my hips up for the body hook.

With Albert's right arm extended, his ribs are vulnerable on his right side. I take advantage of this by rotating my hips in a clockwise direction and hammering a hook to his body.

Before Albert has a chance to recover, I prepare to throw a left uppercut straight up the middle.

My uppercut collides with Albert's chin, lifting his head up and exposing his jaw for the right cross.

I finish the counter combination by rotating my hips in a counterclockwise directing and throwing a right cross to Albert's jaw.

THE STAND UP GAME

COUNTERING RIGHT CROSS TO TAKEDOWN

If your opponent throws a jab, you can almost guarantee that he will follow up with a cross—it's that common of a combination. Ideally, you want to slip your opponent's jab and shoot right in for the takedown because it allows you to avoid dealing with the cross. However, unless your timing is perfect you won't be able to slip every jab. If you miss your opportunity to slip your opponent's jab and he indeed follows with the cross, slipping it is one of your best options. Personally, I'm accustomed to having my head on my opponent's left side when I shoot in for a double-leg, but because slipping an opponent's cross requires that I move my head all the way across his body, it puts me on his right side. Instead of trying to attempt a double-leg from this position, I will usually just tie him up in a body-lock. From the body-lock you can work to take your opponent down or use one of the other techniques I lay out in the upcoming section. I particularly like the technique I show here because I'm using the momentum of the slip and my opponent's compromised positioning to get the takedown.

I'm in a standard fighting stance, squared off with Paco in the pocket.

As Paco throws a straight right cross, I slip his punch by turning my shoulders and hips in a counterclockwise direction. Notice how this movement resembles the movement you make when throwing a cross of your own.

The instant I slip the punch, I drop my level and push off my right foot. This allows me to close the distance between us and lock Albert up in a body-lock.

Continuing to drive forward, I lock my hands together around Paco's waist. It is important to notice the positioning of my hands—they are digging into the soft portion of Paco's midsection, just below his ribs and above his hip.

I continue my forward progression by stepping my left foot to the outside of Paco's right leg. Not only does this allow me to trip him, but it also prevents him from stepping back and reestablishing his base.

Squeezing the body-lock tight and driving my weight into Paco, I take him to the ground. Notice how I step my right leg over his body—this allows me to instantly claim the mount position.

Keeping my body-lock tight, I claim the mount position. From here I can work from the mount or work to take Paco's back. Choosing which option to utilize depends largely upon how your opponent reacts to the takedown.

COUNTERING THE CROSS

COUNTER LEFT CROSS TO DOUBLE-LEG TAKEDOWN

The only time I shoot for a double-leg takedown on a southpaw fighter is when he throws a left cross and I manage to slip it. The reason it works so well is because the cross squares up my opponent's hips, making his back leg reachable. It also puts my head on the outside of his left arm, which makes it difficult for him to block my shot. Going for the double-leg on a southpaw when his hips aren't squared is hard to manage. The single is a much better option because his front leg is right there.

I'm in a standard fighting stance, squared off with Paco in the pocket.

As Paco throws a left cross, I slip his punch by dropping my level, slightly rotating my hips and shoulders in a clockwise direction, and placing the majority of my weight on my right leg.

As Paco's punch sails by the side of my head, I push off my right leg to close the distance and then wrap both arms around the back of his legs. It is important to note that I am not slipping the punch and then shooting in. As I'm slipping, I'm already moving into position to execute the double-leg.

I step my right foot forward, planting it to the outside of Paco's left leg.

Driving off my right foot, I cut the corner and step my left foot to the outside of Paco's right leg. As I drive to my left, he quickly loses balance and begins falling to the mat.

I follow Paco to the mat and pin him up against the cage.

SLIPPING THE HOOK

The hook is a difficult strike to spot because it approaches from the side rather than straight on. It's also a difficult strike to evade because it often requires dropping down into a crouched stance, which involves moving your whole body. However, if you manage to slip your opponent's hook, you'll most likely get the takedown. If you sense the double-leg will be hard to achieve because the momentum of your opponent's hook staggered his hips, obtaining a body-lock and working for the takedown from there is a good alternative.

I'm in a standard fighting stance, squared off with Albert in the pocket.

As Albert throws a left hook, I slip his punch by dropping down into a crouched stance.

Once Albert's hook clears my head, I pop back up into my standard stance.

SLIPPING THE HOOK TO 3 PUNCH COMBO

When you slip an opponent's hook, a lot of times the momentum of his punch will carry his body around, opening his entire midsection for an attack. In such a situation, a good option is to send a powerful hook to his kidney. If you land with any kind of force, your opponent's body will defensively coil into your fist. As you already know, I like to follow this up with an uppercut because there is almost always an opening to land it. The uppercut lifts my opponent's head, making him vulnerable to the always devastating left hook. I've ended the sequence on this last punch, but you can always keep coming with more—a right cross, a double-leg takedown, whatever.

I'm in a standard fighting stance, squared off with Albert in the pocket.

As Albert throws a left hook, I slip his punch by dropping down into a crouched stance.

As the hook soars past my head, I chamber my right hand and prepare to throw a right body hook to Albert's kidney.

I land a right body shot to Albert's kidney. He immediately reacts by coiling his body into my fist, creating an opening for the right uppercut.

I come straight up the middle with a right uppercut. This rocks Albert's head back, creating an opening for the left hook.

I immediately follow the uppercut with a left hook to the right side of Albert's face.

CATCH AND GO COMBO TO TAKEDOWN

When an opponent launches an attack, your ideal reaction should be to slip his strike and then immediately come forward with an attack of your own. It's ideal, but not always possible. If your opponent is a proficient striker it will be very difficult to slip every one of his strikes. The chances are he will pay close attention to your footwork and movement, waiting for the moment when you are off balance or stretched out to launch his attack. If you find yourself in a situation where a strike is coming at you and you're out of position to slip it, your next best option is to block the strike. However, assuming a purely defensive posture can get you in trouble, as Tito Ortiz learned when he faced Chuck Liddell in UFC 47. He covered up to block Liddell's punches, but that only led to more punches. Eventually one sneaked through Ortiz's defenses. In order to avoid such an outcome when blocking a strike, a good tactic is to employ something I call "catch and go." When an opponent attacks, you want to catch his attack by blocking his punch, and then immediately fire back with the same hand you blocked his punch with. The combination you choose to put together depends largely upon your game plan and opponent. I included the technique below not because it is something to live by, but rather to get your creative juices flowing.

I'm in a standard fighting stance, squared off with Troy in the pocket.

Troy throws a left hook at my face, but I'm out of position to slip it. To avoid getting hit, I block the hook by keeping my right hand pressed tight against the right side of my face. It is important that you keep your arm snug against your face to prevent the punch from knocking your arm into your head, and it is also important to keep your arm tightly coiled to close any gaps the punch might be able to sneak through.

Catching Troy's hook with my right arm, I fire a cross before he has a chance to bring his left hand back and block the punch. It is important to notice that I am following a line of attack based off the punch Troy threw. If he had thrown a different punch, I would have followed a different line of attack.

Because I immediately countered with the cross, my fist collides with Troy's chin before he can bring his left arm back to block it.

Having discombobulated Troy with the cross, I immediately follow up with a left hook. The moment Troy sees it coming out of his peripheral vision, his natural reaction is to keep his hands up to block a potential barrage.

Thinking I'm going to unleash with more strikes, Troy keeps his hands up to protect his face. Capitalizing on his reaction, I drop my level, explode off my right foot to cover the distance between us, and wrap both arms around the back of his legs. From here I will complete the double-leg takedown by cutting the corner (p. 30).

SLIPPING THE HOOK TO BODY CLINCH

When your opponent throws a hook, his fist and shoulders move along a circular path rather than a linear path, which means you must avoid the strike differently than you would either a jab or cross. You have a couple of different options depending upon the situation. If you can spot the hook the instant your opponent begins to throw it, you can drop your elevation and shoot in for the double-leg takedown because his hips will still be squared up. However, as your opponent's fist and body progress along their circular trajectory, his hips become less square, making the double-leg takedown harder to accomplish. In such a scenario, a good approach is to drop into a crouched stance, let the punch sail over your head, and then step forward and establish a body-lock, which is the technique I show here. Once you've established a body-lock, you can work for the takedown or choose a number of other options. To learn those options, visit the "Clinch" section.

I'm in a standard fighting stance, squared off with Paco in the pocket.

As Paco throws a left hook, I begin dropping my level to evade the punch.

Having dropped down into a crouched stance, Paco's hook sails over my head.

The momentum of Paco's punch carries his body in a clockwise direction, exposing his back. Immediately I explode off my right leg, step my left foot between his legs, and wrap both arms around his waist, securing a double under-hook body-lock.

Stepping my right foot to the outside of Paco's left leg, I dig my grip into the soft tissue just above his hip and below his ribs. From here you have several options, such as picking your opponent up and slamming him down. To review these options, visit the clinch section.

COUNTERING KICKS

COUNTERING KICK TO TAKEDOWN

In this technique I'm countering my opponent's kick by shooting forward the instant I see him set his kick into motion. Timing is obviously crucial. The goal is to close the distance before the kick lands. If you can manage this, you will greatly reduce the impact of your opponent's kick and catch him on one leg, making the takedown effortless.

I'm in a standard fighting stance, squared off with Paco in the pocket.

I see Paco snap his hips in a counterclockwise direction to throw a right roundhouse kick. Immediately I begin to drop my level and shoot in.

As I shoot in, I maneuver my head to Paco's right side and snatch up his kick with my left hand. Because I closed the distance so quickly and grabbed a hold of the kick, I not only smothered the impact of the blow, but I also caught Paco off balance, making the takedown significantly easier to manage.

With the power of the kick lost, I lock my hands together behind Paco's back—securing the double under-hooks—and step my right foot to the outside of his left leg.

As I step my left leg forward, Paco loses his balance and is forced to the ground.

I follow Paco to the mat, staying as tight to him as possible to prevent him from scrambling.

COUNTERING KICK TO SWEEP-KICK TAKEDOWN

Catching an opponent's kicks is not something that you should look for—it's something that just sort of happens. The reason you shouldn't look for it is because if your opponent sees that you're trying to catch all of his kicks, he will use your reactions against you. He might fake a kick and then throw a punch as you drop your arm. He might throw a few kicks toward your ribs, get you comfortable with dropping your arm to catch them, and then throw a kick to your head. Unless you are an experienced Muay Thai practitioner, it can be difficult to tell the difference between a rib kick and a head kick, and the last thing you want is to catch a shin across the side of your neck. Usually the only time I will catch an opponent's kick is when I can't get out of the way in time or if I am too slow rushing in for the takedown. Once you have caught the kick, it is important to wrap it up tight so he can't pull it free, just like you would when going for an ankle lock. Your opponent will have very little balance, and to topple him over all you have to do is kick his planted leg out from underneath him. If your goal is to bring the fight to the ground, you can do this the moment you snatch up his leg. If you're in no rush to bring the fight down or want to keep the fight standing, you can unload from this position with an assortment of strikes, including punches to his face, knees to his body, or kicks to his planted leg.

I'm in a standard fighting stance, squared off with Paco in the pocket.

Reading Paco's movements, I see that he is about to throw a right roundhouse kick. Immediately I throw my right hand forward to push Paco off balance and eliminate some of the power behind his kick. I also begin dropping my left arm in preparation to catch his leg. If you're uncertain as to whether or not the kick is headed toward your ribs, a better approach is to check your opponent's kick.

Pushing on Paco's chest with my right hand, I eliminate some of the power behind his kick. This not only makes the impact less painful, but it also makes it easier for me to secure his leg, which I do by hooking my left arm around the outside of his right leg.

Squeezing my left arm tight around Paco's leg, I take a step forward with my right foot and drive him backwards with my right hand.

As my weight comes down onto my right foot, I kick/sweep Paco's left leg out from underneath him, sending him to the mat.

As Paco lands on his back, I keep my left arm hooked around his right leg for control. From here I can begin working to pass his guard.

CHECK TO OVERHAND

You need to know how to deal with an opponent's leg kicks, and for me the answer is to check his kick and then throw a powerful overhand right. You certainly have the option of getting out of the way of the kick, but then you won't be in range to strike back. Personally, I like to make my opponent pay. The important part is to catch your opponent while he is kicking or in the process of recovering from the kick. If your opponent catches you off guard and you don't have time to check, just plant your weight on your lead leg and throw.

I'm squared up with Paco in kicking range.

Paco steps in to throw a right roundhouse kick to my left leg.

I block Paco's low kick by bringing my left leg slightly off the ground and catching the kick with my shin.

I drive my left leg to the mat, using that forward momentum to fuel an overhand right.

Before Paco can retract his right leg and reestablish his stance, I step my left foot down to the mat, swing my hips in a counterclockwise direction, and throw the overhand right.

Continuing to press forward, I sneak my overhand punch around Paco's guard.

COUNTERING THE TAKEDOWN

Although you should always head into a fight with an offensive mind-set, understanding how to block your opponent's takedowns by sprawling, as well as understanding all of your options off the sprawl, is critical for both the striker and grappler. Strikers obviously want to avoid getting put on their back because they lose their ability to make the most out of their punches and kicks. Grapplers want to avoid getting taken down because the majority of MMA competitors are now well versed in submissions, making it much more difficult to finish an opponent from your back. Every once in a while a grappler lying on the canvas will throw up a triangle and get the finish, but it doesn't happen nearly as often as it used to. Most of the time he gets dragged over to the fence and absorbs a barrage of downward punches and elbows. In such a situation, his survival often comes down to his ability to escape to a top position or climb to his feet.

Sprawling is a basic wrestling technique that you must incorporate into your offensive game. Learning how to sprawl and execute all of your options off the sprawl takes time and practice. You must incorporate sprawling while sparring, shadow boxing, and hitting the heavy bag and mitts. It also helps to practice a sparring drill where your partner's only goal is to throw strikes and go for a takedown, and your only goal is to throw strikes and defend against the takedown. As your opponent constantly drops his level, you'll slowly learn how to differentiate between a real shot and a fake one that is used to create an opening to strike. You must also learn how to move laterally. Constantly employing side to side movement not only makes it difficult for your opponent to zero in on you for the takedown, but it will also create openings for you to attack.

Once you understand the dynamics of the sprawl, you must then work tirelessly on developing your timing. The first step to accomplishing this is becoming a master at reading your opponent's movements. Every time your opponent drops his level, he is putting himself into a position from which he can shoot in. However, if you sprawl the instant your opponent drops his level, he still has the option of abandoning the takedown and firing away with punches. To keep this from happening, you simply want to drop your level the moment your opponent drops his. Instead of sprawling, you're mirroring your opponent's movement with your hands up. If your opponent pops back up into a standard stance, you still have the base and balance to come up with him. If he decides to shoot in from his crouched stance, your level is already dropped, making it easy to kick your legs back for the sprawl. The tricky part is not only spotting the exact instant that your opponent commits to the takedown by penetrating in for the shot, but also executing a flawless sprawl in that exact same instant. Learning how to spot that commitment and then react to it is not something that you can learn from reading a book; it can only be developed through experience and a lot of mat time. If you don't put in your dues, you'd best become a master at fighting off your back because that's probably where you will be spending a lot of your time.

Countering the Single-leg

When an opponent shoots in and manages to secure both of your legs for the double, there is a large probability that you'll end up on your back. This isn't true when an opponent snatches up one of your legs for the single. Although the single is easier for him to acquire, you have a lot of options to escape. The first step to defending against the single is developing exceptional balance. In training I'll have a partner snatch up my leg and then run me around the cage. As he tries to take me down, I maintain balance by hopping on one foot. If you can maintain that balance, your options are great. You can sock your opponent in his unprotected face, as well as execute one of the techniques I've included in the upcoming section to either break his hold or use his hold against him and take him to the ground, putting you in the top position. Having developed good single-leg defense has saved me from ending up on my back in many, many fights.

PUSH AWAY TAKEDOWN DEFENSE

Pushing an opponent off you as he shoots in is the most basic way to defend against a takedown. Instead of stopping your opponent's shot with your body, you step off to the side and allow his momentum to carry him forward into the open air. It's kind of like a bullfighter and his red cape. If you execute this technique a couple of times on an opponent who knows his only chance of victory is bringing the fight to the ground, there is a good chance that he will start to get desperate. He might start shooting in at awkward moments with sloppy shots or swinging wildly in hopes of knocking you out. Becoming a master at stopping your opponent's shots can open up a plethora of opportunity.

I'm in my fighting stance, squared off with Reagan.

As Reagan steps forward with a jab, I parry it with my right hand.

Immediately following the jab, Reagan drops his level and shoots in for the takedown. As he tries closing the distance, I dig my left forearm into the left side of his neck. This prevents him from getting the penetration he needs for the takedown.

Keeping my left forearm dug into the left side of Reagan's neck, I step my left foot back and allow his momentum to continue forward.

Pivoting my body in a counterclockwise direction, I push Reagan away before he can regain his base.

PUSH AWAY TAKEDOWN DEFENSE TO KNEE

When an opponent shoots in for a takedown his head obviously drops, and this gives you an opportunity to land a powerful knee to his face. You can catch your opponent with a knee as he reaches for your legs, you can defend his takedown with a sprawl and then land the knee while he is pinned underneath you, or you can avoid the takedown by stepping to the side as you did in the previous technique and then throwing a knee while your opponent is off balance, which is the technique I demonstrate here. I like this technique in particular because when an opponent shoots in he is mentally and physically prepped to collide with your body. When you avoid that collision by pushing off him and stepping to the side, it throws him off balance. You can take advantage of that opening by landing a knee as I do below, but you can also land a punch or go for a takedown. Deciding what to do depends upon your goals in the fight and the techniques you are most proficient with.

I'm squared up with Reagan in a standard stance.

Reagan drops his level and shoots in for a takedown.

I evade the attack by posting my left hand on Reagan's head, stepping my left leg back, and pivoting in a counterclockwise direction on my right foot. Reagan misses his target and is cast off balance as a result.

I take advantage of Reagan's compromised positioning by driving a left knee into his head.

I pushed a stunned Reagan back and prepare to set up my next attack.

BASIC SPRAWL

When an opponent shoots in for a takedown, it's always good to catch his shot before he gets deep and then simply step out of the way. This is ideal, but not always possible. If you're in the pocket exchanging punches and your opponent suddenly drops and shoots in, you won't always have the time or room to step to the side and avoid the collision. In order not to get taken down, you must have an excellent sprawl. The form of your sprawl should be based upon the amount of penetration your opponent gets. If his shot isn't that deep, you can stay up on your toes. But if his shot is deep and you remain on your toes, your opponent will be able to get underneath your hips, snatch up your legs, and mow you over to your back. To stop this from happening, you want to flatten out so that your hips and the top of your feet are lying flat on the canvas. This is key. If your hips are flat, it traps your opponent underneath you and makes it much harder for him to snatch up your legs. It is also wise to pummel your arms underneath your opponent's arms as he gets his penetration. This will hold his body at bay and trap his head underneath you, which prevents him from sneaking out to the side and finishing the double-leg takedown. The proper form is to have one elbow locked down to your ribs, your opponent's head in the center of your body, and your other hand on his arm for control.

I'm standing in my standard fighting stance.

I drop my level into a crouched stance.

Keeping my right foot posted on the ground, I place my palms on the mat and drop my left leg back.

I immediately shoot my right leg back and drop my hips flat to the mat. It is important to notice how I turn my hips and rotate my shoulders. This helps drive my weight down into my opponent. It is also very important to notice that I am not up on my toes. The tops of my feet are lying flat on the mat. This allows me to get my hips as low as possible, as well as prevents me from popping back up if my opponent should continue to drive forward.

SPRAWL TO TURTLE TRANSITION

When you sprawl and your opponent takes no immediate action to escape the bottom position, you have several options. If the event you're fighting in allows knees to the head, you can dish out some damage. You could also attempt a submission such as the guillotine, but these days fighters are getting very good at protecting their neck in the north/south sprawl position. Since I want to keep the fight on the ground, my favorite option is to circle around my opponent and obtain the turtle position the moment I sprawl. Not only does this open up a number of different strikes, but it also gives me the option of working to take my opponent's back.

I'm in a standard fighting stance, squared off with Paco in the pocket.

Paco throws a left jab. In addition to slipping his punch, I also parry it with my right hand and guide it past my head.

Right off the jab Paco drops his level and shoots in for a double-leg takedown.

I stuff his shot by catching his shoulder in the crook of my left elbow and dropping my left leg back. Notice how the top of my left foot is flat on the mat. If Paco should continue to drive forward, this would allow my body to slide backwards on the top of my foot rather than pop back up, which tends to happen when you're on the ball of your foot. When you pop up, you give your opponent the space he needs to get under your hips and finish the takedown.

As Paco continues to drive forward for the double, I slide back on the top of my foot and drop my hips flat to the ground. The moment you get your hips all the way down, your opponent will no longer be able to complete the takedown.

Wasting no time, I reach my right hand around Paco's back and begin to circle my body in a counterclockwise direction.

Maintaining downward pressure on Paco's back, I continue to circle in a counterclockwise direction. Then I come up onto my right knee.

I establish the turtle position by rotating my body so that my right side is digging into Paco's back. Although I'm preparing to land some punches to his head, my main goal will be to get my hooks in and secure his back so I can finish the fight.

SPRAWL TO STANDING OPTION

There are a few things that you can do to increase your chance of successfully sprawling when your opponent shoots in for the takedown. The first is to constantly monitor his tendencies. A lot of grapplers who want nothing to do with stand-up will work their way into the pocket with a jab or a string of jabs and then take their shot. If you realize your opponent wants to take the fight down, expect each one of his strikes to be followed by a takedown and constantly employ side-to-side movement. A good wrestler can shoot in from outside of striking range, but it becomes much harder for him to aim that shot in the correct direction when you are always moving. If your opponent has excellent "striking to the takedown" combinations, you're going to have your work cut out for you. With such opponents it is often hard to side-step and avoid the collision, so you must practice getting your hips flat to the ground to stuff his shot. Once you've accomplished that, you have several options. If you want the fight standing, you might want to work back to your feet utilizing this technique. If you want the fight on the ground, you will want to secure the top position as I did in the previous technique.

Paco has shot in for a takedown and I stuffed his shot by sprawling. My left arm is to the left side of his head, my legs are back, and I'm pressing my weight down on top of him. It is important to notice that the top of my left foot is lying flat on the mat. In addition to allowing my hips to get all the way down to the mat, positioning my foot in this way will also allow my entire body to slide backwards if Paco should continue to drive forward for the takedown. If I were up on the ball of my foot and Paco drove forward, my foot would stick to the mat and my hips would inevitably rise, allowing Paco to complete the takedown.

Now that I've stopped Paco's forward momentum with my sprawl, I come up onto my knees. Notice how I still have my left arm hooked over Paco's shoulder. This prevents him from driving in again and attempting to complete the takedown as I rise back to my feet.

I continue to work back to my feet by posting my hands and left foot on the mat.

Posting on my left foot, I place my hands on Paco's left shoulder to keep him at bay.

Pushing Paco away with my hands, I come up to my feet.

I return to my standard stance and search for an opening to launch an attack.

HIGH KNEES FROM SPRAWL CONTROL

It's ideal to catch your opponent in a front headlock as you stuff his shot with a sprawl because you can immediately start dropping knees. However, sometimes your arm will end up on the wrong side of your opponent's head. In such a situation, keep your weight pressed down on your opponent and quickly maneuver your arm around his head and secure a front headlock. Once you get it, pick your butt up as high as you can to create as much distance as possible. If you don't create that distance, you're likely to get all jammed up and end up hitting your opponent's head with your thigh rather than your knee. You also want to make your knee as sharp as possible and really drive it in. You can even try cutting an angle to land harder shots. If you're a striker and your opponent is relentless on completing the takedown, you might want to land a couple of knees and then work back to your feet if you don't get the knockout. If you're a grappler, you may want to land a couple of knees and then run around and take his back.

Here I am demonstrating how to grip your opponent's head when you capture him in the north/south sprawl control position. I cup my right hand underneath Reagan's chin, and then wrap my right arm around the left side of his head.

Coming up onto my feet, I elevate my hips above my shoulders. I then drive my weight through my right shoulder and into Reagan's upper back.

Keeping the front headlock tight and continuing to drive my weight down into Reagan's back, I lift my right leg high into the air.

Still applying downward pressure with my body, I drive my right knee straight down into the top of Reagan's head. It is important to note that as I drop my knee, I use my control grip to pull Reagan's head into the strike. This prevents Reagan from being able to pull away as the knee lands.

STRAIGHT KNEES FROM SPRAWL CONTROL

This is another way you can land knee strikes from the front headlock position. In the previous technique I hoisted my leg as high as I could and then came down with a devastating strike. In this technique, I'm pulling my knee back and coming straight in. It doesn't pack as much power, but it tends to have better speed and accuracy. Deciding which technique to use depends upon the situation. Your opponent will have one hand to defend your knee strikes, and if you're having a hard time landing knees from above, you can switch the trajectory of your knees and come straight in. Usually what ends up happening is you use a combination of both knee strikes. You might lift one leg up high, making your opponent think your knee will come barreling down, and then you execute a quick switch-step and throw your opposite knee straight in. It is important when throwing the straight knee that you don't simply power your leg forward; you also want to use the front headlock to pull your opponent's head into your knee. It really helps beef up the power behind your shots. You also want to make sure to keep your hips up because it allows you to maintain downward pressure on your opponent and keep him pinned beneath you.

I secured the front headlock position on Albert. My left hand is cupped underneath his chin, my left arm is wrapped around the right side of his head, I'm up on my feet, my hips are held high, and I'm driving my weight down through my left shoulder and into Albert's back to keep him pinned to the mat.

I fake a right knee strike by lifting my right leg off the canvas.

As Albert prepares to defend against a right knee, I drop my right foot to the mat.

The moment my right foot comes down, I throw my left leg straight back.

As my left knee strike nears Albert's head, I do two things at once. I lift his face by pulling up on his chin, which gives me a better target, and I pull his entire head into my knee to ensure he doesn't back out before the knee lands.

With my left leg coiled tight, I crash my knee into Albert's head.

I quickly pull my left leg back to prevent Albert from latching onto it.

SPRAWL CONTROL

SPRAWL CONTROL TO SIDE CONTROL KNEES

This is another option you can choose from the sprawl control position. Instead of angling around your opponent and assuming the turtle position, here you angle around him and force him over to his back so you can assume side control. Although it depends upon the person, obtaining side control tends to be a little more secure than the turtle position because it is harder for your opponent to stand up and he doesn't have the option of rolling into guard. Once in side control, throwing knees is a good option because you have control of your opponent's head and one of his legs, which limits his defense.

I secured the front headlock position on Reagan. My right hand is cupped underneath his chin, my right arm is wrapped around the left side of his head, I'm up on my feet, my hips are held high, and I'm driving my weight down through my right shoulder and into Reagan's back to keep him pinned to the mat.

In order to transition to side control, I need to turn the corner. I do this by stepping my left leg in a clockwise direction.

Still circling in a clockwise direction around Reagan, I slide my right leg toward my left and then come down onto my right knee. As I do this, I force my head underneath Reagan's body.

I reach my left hand around Reagan's right leg and pull it out from underneath him. As I do this, I drive off my left foot and push my weight into him, forcing him over onto his side.

Dropping down to my knees, I hook my left arm all the way around Reagan's right leg for control and then distribute my weight over his body to prevent him from scrambling.

Keeping my arms locked tight and my weight pressed down, I raise my right leg high into the air.

Controlling Reagan with my weight and arms, I drop a right knee to his head.

BACK TO STANDING OFF DOUBLE-LEG TAKEDOWN

If your opponent shoots in and you don't manage to sprawl in time, you want to avoid landing flat on your back because you will most likely get stuck there. When I get taken down, I'll do everything in my power to land on my side. From there, I will post one hand on the mat and push on my opponent's head with my other hand. When done quickly, it allows me to pull my legs out from underneath him and stand right back up. If you manage to block the majority of your opponent's shots, as well as quickly pop up every time he takes you down, it starts messing with his head, especially if he wants nothing to do with your stand-up skills. He'll start thinking, "Man, I can't take this guy to the ground." Meanwhile, you're just landing unreal punches to his face.

I'm in a standard fighting stance, squared off with Beach.

As Beach throws a left jab at my face, I parry it with my right hand.

Immediately following the jab, Beach shoots in for a double-leg takedown.

Wrapping up my legs, Beach uses his forward momentum to drive me to the ground.

As I fall back, I purposely land on my right side and keep my shoulders elevated off the mat.

Planting my right hand on the mat and my left hand on Beach's right shoulder, I immediately begin to scoot my hips back to free my right leg from underneath Beach's body.

Pulling my right leg out from underneath Beach's body, I use my posted right hand to pop up to my feet.

Using my left arm to gauge distance, I stand all the way up.

I step back and assume my standard fighting stance.

HAND-CLASP GUILLOTINE OFF DOUBLE-LEG

Ideally you want to execute a flawless sprawl when your opponent shoots in, but you don't always have the time or room to get your hips down and your legs back. In such a situation going for the guillotine can sometimes be a good option. If you can gain control of your opponent's head before he wraps up both of your legs, then you have a chance to not only defend against the takedown, but also finish the fight. It is important to pay attention to the pictures below because this guillotine is done a little differently than the traditional one. With the hand-clasp guillotine, you want to cup both hands underneath your opponent's chin, dig the sharp part of your wrist into his throat, lift up with your arms, and drive your belly button into your opponent's head. The standard guillotine still works, but your opponent usually won't expect the hand-clasp guillotine. This element of surprise makes the submission difficult to defend against and often results in a quick tap.

Albert shoots in for a double-leg takedown, catching me off guard. Realizing I don't have enough time to execute a proper sprawl, I decide to catch him in a guillotine choke. I begin by hooking my right hand underneath his chin and steering his head toward the center of my stomach as he comes forward.

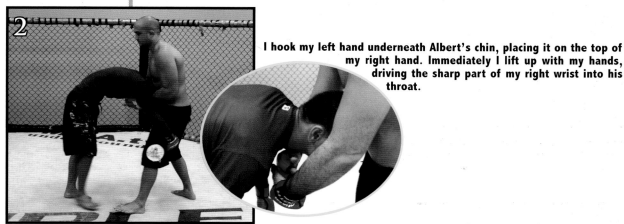

I hook my left hand underneath Albert's chin, placing it on the top of my right hand. Immediately I lift up with my hands, driving the sharp part of my right wrist into his throat.

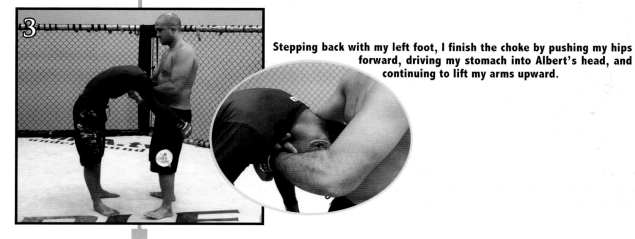

Stepping back with my left foot, I finish the choke by pushing my hips forward, driving my stomach into Albert's head, and continuing to lift my arms upward.

GUILLOTINE CHOKE TO GUARD

Although the guillotine choke isn't my favorite submission, it's responsible for ending many fights. As I have already mentioned, a lot of opponents will set up their takedowns off strikes or evade one of your punches and shoot in, making it difficult to defend against the takedown by angling out to the side or sprawling. When this happens, you should pay attention to your opponent's form. Many fighters shoot in with their head down. If your opponent does this, you can wrap your arm around his head and apply a guillotine choke. There are two things you must achieve for the choke to work. You must secure the choke the moment you come down onto your back—you never want to willingly go to your back unless you're confident the choke will end the fight—and you must capture your opponent between your legs in the guard position. Just as with the previous technique, this is not something you look for. The option just sort of presents itself in the chaos of battle.

Paco shoots in for a double-leg takedown, catching me off guard. Instantly I see that his hands are low and his neck is exposed, making him susceptible to a guillotine choke.

It's too late to get my hips back and catch Paco underneath my sprawl, so I quickly maneuver my left arm around his head and slide my wrist across his neck. Notice that I have positioned my legs to the outside of Paco's legs. When I go down, this will ensure that I can capture him in my guard, which is pivotal for finishing the choke.

As Paco drives me to the ground, I wrap my legs around his waist to capture him in my guard. At the same time, I bring my right arm around to the front of his shoulder. Then I secure the guillotine choke position by gripping my hands together. It is important to notice that my right arm is not reaching underneath Paco's left arm—my arm is in front of his shoulder.

As my back comes down onto the mat, I interlock my feet and push Paco away from me using my legs. At the same time, I squeeze my arms to lock the choke tight. It is important to note that I'm not pulling my arms straight back. Instead, I am twisting my body slightly in a clockwise direction. This allows me to really tighten up the choke and ensures that my opponent either taps under the pressure or passes out.

KNEE TO SINGLE-LEG DEFENSE

As you probably know by now, it's much easier to defend against a single-leg takedown than a double-leg takedown, so whenever possible you want to avoid having to defend against the double. With this in mind, your best bet for landing a strike as an opponent shoots in without compromising too much is to throw a knee with your lead leg. If your timing is dead on, you might get the knockout, but if it doesn't land flush and your opponent scoops up your lead leg, all you have to defend is the single-leg takedown. Once you throw that knee a couple of times, your opponent will become a lot more hesitant to shoot in, and this not only makes his takedowns easier to block, but also easier to see coming. However, landing the front knee requires perfect timing, and timing can only come about through lots of practice. A good drill is to put on a massive kneepad and have one of your training partner throw on a helmet. Start by having your training partner shoot in at a very slow speed, but once you become comfortable throwing your front knee, pick the pace up until you're going at full speed. After you get good with this technique, you'll want to use it in a fight, but unless you want to get put on your back, you must always remember that your first priority is defending against the takedown. Unless you have an extreme amount of confidence in your ability to block the single-leg, sprawling and catching your opponent underneath you is always a better option.

I'm in a standard fighting stance, squared off with Paco in the pocket.

The instant I see Paco drop his level and shoot in for a double-leg takedown, I lift my left knee toward his face and drive my hips forward.

My left knee collides with Paco's chin.

Stunned but not knocked out, Paco wraps up my left leg before I can pull it back to the ground. Although I have avoided the double-leg takedown, I now have to defend the single-leg takedown.

As soon as Paco traps my left leg, I immediately eliminate much of his control by maneuvering my head to the left side of his head. From here I will work to take Paco down with a counter or work to free my leg by driving punches into his face (p. 86).

PUNCHING YOUR LEG FREE

When an opponent shoots in and hauls your lead leg off the ground, a good tactic to avoid the takedown is to find your balance and land a string of punches to his unprotected face. The idea is to bother him so much with strikes that he forgets all about the takedown. Once you get your opponent to abandon the single-leg, push off of him and reset your base. The key to success with this technique is to think about positioning first and striking second. If your opponent drives in, you want to hop back and maintain your balance. If you think about striking first and positioning second, you might land a few punches, but eventually your opponent will compromise your balance and take you down.

I'm balancing on one leg, defending the single-leg takedown. It is important to maintain tension in your trapped leg, as well as have your shin wedged up between your opponent's legs. This helps to ensure that when your opponent moves, your leg won't move independently from your body. If your trapped leg is relaxed and your opponent pulls on it, your leg will move independently and eventually whip your body off balance.

Maintaining balance on my right leg, I control Reagan's head with my left arm and drive a right uppercut into his left eye socket.

I wind up for another uppercut.

I land yet another uppercut to Reagan's left eye socket.

Blind and frustrated, Reagan loosens his grip on my left leg. Immediately I maneuver my head to the right side of Reagan's head, stripping him of the positioning he needs to finish the single-leg takedown.

Bringing my elbows in tight to my body and pinching Reagan's arms together with my hands, I regain my base and posture and drive my left leg to the ground.

Although I have escaped the single-leg, I continue to push Reagan's arms together with my hands to avoid getting punched as I back out.

Backing away, I continue to control Reagan's arms to avoid getting hit. From here I will return to my standard fighting stance and begin to set up an attack.

HAND-CLASP GUILLOTINE OFF SINGLE

In a previous technique I demonstrated how to defend against the double-leg takedown using the hand-clasp guillotine, and here I'm demonstrating how to use it to defend against the single-leg. The moment you wrap up your opponent's neck, he will be forced to start defending against the choke, which takes his focus away from completing the single. From there you will either be able to finish the choke or your opponent will defend against the choke and you'll escape the single-leg. Either way, you win.

Reagan has my left leg trapped, and he is working for a single-leg takedown.

I maneuver my left leg to the outside of Reagan's right leg and push down on his head with my right hand. Notice how I am repositioning his head to the center of my torso.

Balancing on my right leg, I slide my left hand under Reagan's chin. Then I slide my right hand under his chin and over the top of my left hand. After completing these two actions, I drive my weight down on Reagan's head and press my left leg toward the mat.

By driving my weight and left leg downward, I break Reagan's grip and place my left foot on the mat. To finish the hand clasp guillotine, I curl my left wrist into Reagan's neck, posture up, and drive my belly button into his head.

DEFENDING THE SINGLE (PUSHING THE HEAD OUT)

To become proficient at defending against the single-leg takedown, you must first learn how to maintain your balance while hopping on one leg. If you dedicate a small amount of time to this during practice each week, you will be surprised at how quickly you can improve with this technique. Once you've perfected the hop around, you must then learn how to disengage or use your opponent's compromised positioning to take him to the ground and obtain the top position. With my primary base being jiu-jitsu, I tend to opt for a takedown. To achieve this, I first work to force my opponent's head down and to the outside of my body. Once I manage that, my opponent's chances of completing the single are slim. To put him on his back, I simply need to scoop up his rear leg and turn his body like a wheel.

Having snatched up my lead leg, Albert attempts to haul me to the ground utilizing a single-leg takedown.

Maintaining balance on my right leg, I push Albert's head to the left side of my body using my hands.

Having moved Albert's head to the outside of my body, I place my left hand on the back of his head and drive it downward. At the same time, I wrap my right arm around the back of his left leg.

Continuing to push Albert's head down with my left hand, I pull his left leg off the ground with my right arm. This circular motion casts his body into a forward roll.

Following Albert to the ground, I clear his legs and land in side control.

THE CLINCH

In mixed martial arts several different types of clinching styles can be utilized: the Muay Thai clinch, the one-arm dirty boxing clinch, and the wrestling clinch. To become proficient in MMA, you must not only understand the core principles of each style, but you must also understand how to blend them together. A fighter who can tie his opponent up in the Muay Thai Clinch, land a couple of knees, and then transition to the wrestling clinch and execute a throw is a lot more dangerous than a fighter who is only proficient with one clinching style.

Because it's nearly impossible to master all clinching styles at the same time, you should first concentrate on the clinch game that you most gravitate toward. If you come from a Muay Thai background or you derive the most enjoyment from training Muay Thai, focusing on the Muay Thai clinch is a good place to start. Once you feel confident with your Thai clinch, start experimenting with the wrestling or dirty boxing clinch to make your game stronger. Not only will this increase your offensive options, but if you should find yourself fighting an opponent who is a wrestler, you'll have an understanding of what his actions and reactions will be. After you have added a number of techniques from a second clinching style, start playing around with the third. The more techniques you add to your base, the more dangerous you become. You will also be a lot more prepared to deal with the numerous scenarios that can occur in MMA competition.

Wrestling Clinch

The wrestling clinch is based largely upon hip and body control, and it's structured around scoring a throw, a body-lock takedown, a double-leg takedown, or a single-leg takedown. The primary battle is to pummel your arms underneath your opponent's arms and secure the double under-hooks, the details of which will be explained in the upcoming section. Generally when playing this clinch you want to keep a low center of gravity so you can shoot in for the takedown, but a lot of Greco Roman wrestlers and Judoka prefer to stand more erect because it better allows them to execute throws. With thousands of dangerous wrestlers entering the sport each year, learning the intricacies of the wrestling clinch is mandatory for survival.

Muay Thai Clinch

The Muay Thai clinch can be a truly devastating position because of the elbow and knee strikes that become available. This clinch is quite different from the wrestling clinch because it is based on head control. Instead of working to pummel your arms underneath your opponent's arms to establish the under-hooks, you're pummeling in for your opponent's head. Once you gain control of your opponent's head, you want to constantly cut angles while pushing and pulling your opponent off balance. This exposes his body and makes him vulnerable to powerful knee strikes.

The Dirty Boxing Clinch

The dirty boxing clinch works wonderfully for wrestlers and of course "dirty boxers" who are used to controlling their opponent's head and striking at the same time. Randy Couture is a perfect example of a fighter who has mastered the dirty boxing clinch. The idea is to gain control of your opponent's head with one arm, and then use that control to push, pull, and jerk your opponent off balance as you deliver punches to his gut and face with your free hand. Wrestlers particularly like this clinch because they retain a base that allows them to quickly drop in for a takedown or execute a throw.

Clinching Drills

It is very important to incorporate clinching drills into your daily training. In order to develop a dangerous clinch game, you must drill and drill and drill. You should be doing pummeling drills, sparring from the clinch with knees, and practicing takedowns from the clinch. You should spend time sparring from the individual clinches, as well as spar utilizing all the clinches together. You should engage in style vs. style matches where you can only use your wrestling clinch against your partner's Muay Thai clinch. Such a drill allows you to feel what is going on, which tells you what you must do to make your style effective against opponents who utilize a different clinching style. Play around as much as possible.

BASIC PUMMELING

Pummeling can be used both offensively and defensively, and learning the nuances of the art is critical for developing a strong clinch game. If you can dominate the pummel, you will have a better chance of achieving your desired goal, whether it be pummeling for a body-lock to take your opponent down or pummeling in to create separation so you can land strikes. The key to developing a strong pummel is to acquire a relaxed tension with your body. If you are too relaxed, your opponent will overpower you. If you are too tense, you will have no sensitivity to your opponent's movements. Learning this fine balance is not something that can be taught through words—you simply have to get into the gym and practice.

I'm tied up with Paco in the body pummel position. This is a neutral position because we both have one under-hook.

To start the pummel for the double under-hooks, I press my right hand flat against my chest and wedge it toward the inside of Paco's left arm. Because Paco also wants to obtain the double under-hooks, he is doing the same exact thing on the left side of my body. Whoever can get the double under-hooks first will have the upper hand.

I maneuver my right hand to the inside of Paco's left arm. Notice how I am hooking my hand around the crook of his elbow.

I push my right arm all the way through, obtaining an under-hook on my right side. I would have the double under-hooks except Paco now has an under-hook on my left side.

In the hunt to obtain the double under-hooks, I begin the process of swimming my left arm through.

I maneuver my left hand to the inside of Paco's right arm, and he swims his left hand to the inside of my right arm.

Paco and I end up back in the neutral position we started in.

PUMMELING TO THE BODY WITH ELBOWS

Being clinched up in the over-under body-lock position is quite common in MMA. The position itself is neutral, so in order to make something happen you need to turn your over-hook into a second under-hook. If you can manage this, then you can synch in the double under-hook body-lock, establish control, and take your opponent to the ground. However, this won't always be easy. In order to pummel in for the under-hook you need to create separation between you and your opponent so you can maneuver your arm to the inside of his arm. The way you create that separation is by moving your head away from the arm you're trying to pummel in. When your opponent feels you do this, he will most likely pummel his opposite arm in to replace his over-hook with an under-hook. As he does this, he too will move his head away from his pummeling arm to create separation. It is at this moment, when both you and your opponent are shifting position, that some striking options become available. Personally, I like to throw an elbow strike. As long as you throw the elbow as you and your opponent are shifting positions, you will not only have the space needed to land the strike, but your opponent's head will also be moving directly into the blow, making it more powerful. Once you land your shot, you should immediately swim your arm back in and continue pummeling for body control.

I'm tied up with Albert in the body pummel position.

I posture up and create the space needed to maneuver my right hand to the inside of Albert's left arm.

As I pummel my right hand underneath Albert's left arm, I angle my right elbow upward.

I throw my right elbow into Albert's left eye.

Following through with the elbow, I swoop my right arm directly underneath Albert's right arm.

I secure an under-hook on my right side.

PUMMELING TO THE BODY WITH KNEES

As I mentioned in the previous technique, every time you pummel in for an under-hook, your opponent is forced to turn his body in that direction in order to establish an under-hook of his own on the opposite side. His action opens a perfect opportunity to land a knee to the body.

I'm tied up with Reagan in the clinch.

I maneuver my right arm to the inside of Reagan's left arm. Notice how I hook my hand around the crook of Reagan's arm.

As I pummel in with my right arm, I drive my right knee into Reagan's mid-section.

I bring my right leg down so that I'm in a southpaw stance.

Immediately I pummel my left arm to the inside of Reagan's right arm.

As I pummel in with my left arm, I drive my left knee into Reagan's mid-section.

I bring my left leg down, putting me in my original stance.

CATCH KNEE TO TAKEDOWN

When pummeling with an opponent in the clinch, the one thing you must really watch out for is dropping your head too far to one side or the other because you become vulnerable to catching a knee to the face. However, every time your opponent throws a knee to your face from the clinch he's creating an opening for you to take him down. If you drop your head inadvertently, this can be hard to manage unless your reactions are lightning quick. But purposely dropping your head to bait your opponent into throwing the knee is another matter. If you do this, you must be prepared to react. The instant your opponent takes the bait, pop back up into your standard stance to avoid the strike, scoop up his lead leg with your arm, heft him off the mat, and slam him down.

I'm tied up with Paco in the body pummel position.

I hunch over and drop my level.

Realizing I have sunk low, Paco throws a left knee at my face.

Seeing the knee coming, I under-hook Paco's left leg with my right arm and posture up to avoid getting hit.

Posturing all the way up, I continue to lift Paco's left leg into the air. As I do this, his right foot lifts off the canvas. I capitalize on his lack of base by shifting the majority of my weight onto my right leg, and then sweeping his right leg out from underneath him with my left leg.

Now that Paco's right foot is off the canvas, I continue to lift his left leg upward. Notice how this turns his body.

As I slam Paco to the canvas, I follow him down to prevent him from scrambling. Notice how I still have my right arm wrapped around his left leg for control.

LEVEL CHANGE TO OUTSIDE KNEE

As you're aware, utilizing combinations that blend striking and grappling techniques is a great way to confuse your opponent and catch him off guard. In this combination, you set your opponent up by dropping your level. Unless your opponent wants to get taken down, the first thing he will do is mirror your movement by dropping his head down to your level. An action is always quicker than a reaction, so for a split second after your opponent drops his head there will be a window of opportunity for you to pop back up and land a knee to his face. However, it is important to be cautious with this technique. If your opponent senses what you're trying to do, he can use the previous technique to catch your leg, lift you off the mat, and slam you down.

I'm tied up with Paco in the body pummel position.

As I drop my level to shoot in, Paco counters by dropping his level.

With Paco's head now within kneeing range, I shoot my left knee upward into his face.

BODY-LOCK TAKEDOWN

Once you establish double under-hooks and secure a body-lock, you can do some serious damage to your opponent. If you have the positioning to lift your opponent off the canvas, slamming him on his head is always a good option. There are many possibilities, so deciding what technique to use depends upon your specialty. This technique is a simple yet effective way to take your opponent down with the double under-hooks and land in the top side-control position.

Having managed to pummel my arms in and secure the double under-hooks, I lock my hands together behind Albert's back.

Keeping my hands locked tight, I step my right foot to the outside of Albert's left leg. This gives me the angle I need to get the takedown.

I begin to rotate my body in a clockwise direction to trip Albert backwards.

Still rotating in a clockwise direction, I use my head and superior positioning to trip Albert backwards.

As Albert falls to his back, I drop to my knees, apply downward pressure to his body to prevent a scramble, and secure the side control position.

GETTING THE HEAD IN OFF DOUBLE UNDER-HOOKS

If your opponent secures the double under-hooks, which you want to avoid at all costs, you're in danger of getting picked up and slammed. To avoid such an outcome, immediately drop your hips and keep a low center of gravity. You also want to relax as much as possible because it is a lot harder to throw something limp than something rigid (if you've ever tried to pick up a drunk friend who is passed out on a curb, you know exactly what I mean). Next you want to get your head underneath your opponent's head. This extends your opponent's arms and pushes your hips back, which allows you to drop your weight a little more and push your way out of the double under-hooks. Adding this technique to your arsenal can get you out of a very tight spot.

Albert has managed to pummel in and secure double under-hooks. In order to avoid getting slammed, I need to create separation between our bodies.

I immediately create separation by placing both hands on Albert's head and pushing it away from me. I also drive my head down into his face. In order to take away the leverage he needs to slam me, I must get my head below his head.

I work my head further down Albert's face to create separation. Pinching my arms together, I plant my right hand on Albert's hip and push him away from me. This breaks his lock, which will allow me to create the space needed to pummel my left arm to the inside of his right arm. It is important to notice that I have dropped my hips down and back, lowering my center of gravity. This steals even more of Albert's leverage.

I pummel my left arm to the inside of Albert's right arm and return to the neutral body pummel position.

ESCAPING UNDER-HOOK CONTROL

If your opponent manages to secure a really deep under-hook when in the clinch, he gains control of that side of your body. When I find myself in this predicament, I place my elbow between my opponent's neck and shoulder, let my arm go limp, and then yank my arm free.

Albert has a tight under-hook on my right side.

To free my right arm, I bring my right elbow up and wedge it between Albert's neck and shoulder.

Keeping my right arm relaxed, I begin to back out and pull my arm free.

I back all the way out.

HIP TOSS (WHIZZER) TO PUNCH

When your opponent has an under-hook and he drives forward for the takedown, you can use his forward momentum against him by utilizing a hip toss. To do this, you rotate your hips, add to his forward momentum by driving your whizzer into his shoulder, and trip him over your leg. Although it is certainly possible to chuck your opponent to the ground with this technique, a lot of opponents will catch themselves before they go down. When this happens, you can use your opponent's compromised positioning to smash a right hand into his face.

Albert presses forward in the body pummel position.

I pivot my body in a clockwise direction to create the angle needed to throw Albert off balance. It is important to mention that I have a tight over-hook with my left arm.

Keeping my left over-hook tight, I maneuver my left leg to the inside of Albert's right leg.

COUNTERING THE UNDER-HOOK

Rotating my hips and shoulders in a clockwise direction, I use my over-hook to drive Albert's upper body downward. At the same time, I kick my left leg straight back. The combination of these actions thrusts Albert forward, toppling his base.

As I bring my left foot back to the canvas, Albert's base is still broken. I take advantage of the opening by socking him in the chin.

PUMMELING FOR THE HEAD TO KNEE

A lot of times when you're pummeling for the body, your opponent will be so focused on obtaining and defending against the double under-hooks, he will forget about his head. This often allows you to bring your arms up and secure the Muay Thai clinch. Once you manage this, a good option is to force your opponent's head down and then drive powerful knees up into his face. If your opponent attempts to pull his head up when you have him in the Thai clinch, he will often forget about his body, which allows you to secure a body-lock. Switching back and forth between pummeling for your opponent's body and head will increase your ability to secure a hold and impose your will.

I'm tied up with Reagan in the body pummel position.

Reagan begins pummeling his left arm toward the inside of my right arm to secure an under-hook.

As Reagan strives for the under-hook on my right side, I reach up and cup my left hand around the back of his head.

Immediately I place my right hand over my left and pinch my elbows together, securing the Muay Thai clinch.

To load up for a knee strike, I step my right foot back, drop my hips, and pull down on Reagan's head.

Still pulling down on Reagan's head, I drive my hips forward and send my right knee crashing into his face.

STRIKING TO HEAD CONTROL

Sometimes when you throw a barrage of strikes at an opponent, he will cover up to block your shots and then freeze in that position. If this happens, you have multiple options. You can hunt for an opening to direct your strikes, shoot in for the takedown, or grab your opponent's head and drive in a couple of knees. It's an excellent time to do some damage. I particularly like throwing a string of punches that ends with a hook. Instead of bringing my hooking hand back, I'll immediately wrap it around the back of my opponent's head, secure the Muay Thai clinch, and then deliver some powerful knees.

I'm squared off with Troy in the pocket.

I throw a straight left jab at Troy's face.

I follow the jab with a straight right cross.

Troy covers up to block my shots, but he makes no attempt to throw strikes of his own. With the ball in my court, I follow the cross with a left hook. Instead of bringing my hooking hand back into my stance, I grip the back of Troy's head with my left hand.

Placing my right hand over my left and pinching my elbows together, I secure the Muay Thai clinch.

Pulling Troy's head down using the Muay Thai clinch, I drive my right knee up into his face.

ELBOW FROM MUAY THAI CLINCH

Anytime you gain control of your opponent's head, you have the ability to land elbow strikes. They can be thrown from the Muay Thai clinch, as well as from the dirty boxing clinch. For the best results, you want to rear back, pull your opponent's head into your elbow with your opposite hand, and then quickly regain control.

I've got Albert in the Muay Thai clinch, giving me control of his head.

Maintaining control of Albert's head with my left hand, I back away just enough to chamber my right elbow.

Pulling Albert's head into me using my left hand, I thrust my right shoulder forward and crash my elbow into the side of his face.

After landing the elbow, I immediately regain control of Albert's head.

HEAD CLINCH TO TAKEDOWN

When you secure the Muay Thai clinch and attempt to pull your opponent's head down to land knee strikes, there is a strong chance that he will strain to keep his head up. If his resistance is great, you can cause his head to snap dramatically back by simply releasing your hold. This creates a small window of opportunity to drop low and shoot in for the takedown.

I've secured the Muay Thai clinch on Troy.

Fearful that I will land a knee to his face, Troy hinders me from pulling his head down by tightening his neck and straightening his posture.

Instead of fighting Troy's resistance, I simply let go of my hold. Because he was applying upward pressure to counter my downward pressure, his head and body straighten the moment I release my grip.

As Troy's head pops up, I drop my level, wrap my arms around the back of his legs, and shoot in for the takedown.

I step forward with my right foot.

Before I can cut the corner, Troy crumbles to the mat. I follow him down and secure the top position.

PUMMELING IN FOR THE HEAD

Gaining control of your opponent's head often requires a pummeling war. If your opponent should happen to get one step ahead of you and gain control of your head, you immediately want to pummel your arms in as I do below to neutralize his advantage. However, if your opponent secures a really tight Thai clinch, making it difficult to pummel your arms to the inside of his arms, you'll want to utilize the next technique in this section. I cannot stress enough the importance of quickly escaping this position. If you do nothing, your opponent has all sorts of options, many of which can put you to sleep.

Albert has secured a Muay Thai clinch, giving him control of my head.

I maneuver my right hand to the inside of Albert's left arm.

Still working my right hand to the inside of Albert's left arm, I begin to maneuver my left arm to the inside of his right arm.

Gripping the back of Albert's head with both hands, I establish control of his head with the Muay Thai clinch.

DESPERATION ESCAPE

When your opponent captures your head in the Muay Thai clinch, your mind should automatically flash a code red alert. How you ended up in such a terrible spot is irrelevant; what matters is escaping the position before you eat a knee to the face. A good way to accomplish this is to jam an arm into your opponent's face, crank his head to the side, and then force him away from you. This creates space and allows you to get the hell out of Dodge.

Having secured the Muay Thai clinch, Albert pulls my head down. I am now vulnerable to numerous attacks, which means I must escape this position quickly.

Bringing my left arm over Albert's right arm, I slide my forearm across his face, which cranks his head to the side. Notice how I drive the outside of my wrist into his jaw. This not only makes the position uncomfortable for him, but it also allows me to push him back and create separation between our bodies.

Creating distance between our bodies by pushing Albert away with my left arm, I maneuver my right arm to the inside of Albert's left arm. I then place my right hand on my left arm. This increases the outward pressure I'm already applying to Albert's face, which creates more separation between our bodies.

By straightening both arms, I push Albert's head back and create the separation needed to escape the position.

As Albert's hands slide off the back of my head, I continue to push him away to prevent him from reestablishing head control.

I fall back into my standard fighting stance.

COUNTERING HEAD CONTROL WITH A TAKEDOWN

When your opponent secures the Muay Thai clinch, it's possible to sneak uppercuts up between his arms and land to his chin, but the chances are his knee strikes will be a lot more powerful than your uppercuts. Instead of trying to bang my way out, I will usually drop my level, get my arms underneath my opponent's arms, and finish with the double under-hook body-lock takedown. If you can't penetrate in for the takedown because your opponent is too strong or has total control, jamming an arm across his face to create separation as I demonstrated in the previous technique is a good backup. It doesn't matter how you escape, just that you do. If you remain in this compromising position for a prolonged period of time, your opponent will most likely find a way to inflict some serious damage.

Reagan has gained control of my head by securing the Muay Thai clinch.

To prevent Reagan from pulling my head down, I immediately drop my level and straighten my back.

I push off my right leg and drive my body straight into Reagan to secure a body-lock.

Securing the double under-hooks, I form a tight body-lock around Reagan's midsection.

Squeezing Reagan in tight with my arms, I drive my head forward.

Still driving forward with my head, I step my right leg to the outside of Reagan's left leg and then rotate my body in a clockwise direction.

Continuing to rotate in a clockwise direction, I drive forward with my head and suck Reagan's body into me using my arms. This forces him to lose balance and he crumbles to the mat.

I keep my body-lock tight as I follow Reagan to the ground.

DIRTY BOXING CLINCH

While the Muay Thai clinch creates openings to land knee strikes, the dirty boxing clinch is built for punches. Personally, I like to use the hand I have wrapped around the back of my opponent's head to either pull his face down into powerful uppercuts or brace his head as I throw repeated hooks. However, you must be careful in this position because your opponent will most likely have one hand wrapped around the back of your head, which means he too has the ability to punch. There have been some epic MMA battles where both fighters just stood their ground and wailed away on each other from the dirty boxing clinch. To avoid such a battle, it's best to hinder your opponent's ability to strike. This can be achieved several different ways. You can circle around him to disrupt his balance as you throw punches. You can control his head with your left arm for a few moments, and then switch and control his head with your right arm. You can push, pull, and jerk his head around as you strike, and you can switch things up by transitioning from the dirty boxing clinch to other dominant clinch positions such as the double under-hooks or head control. There are a lot of wrestlers out there such as Randy Couture who have become masters at destroying their opponents from the dirty boxing clinch, so at the very least you need a basic understanding of this style.

I've assumed the dirty boxing clinch by hooking my left hand around the back of Albert's head and hooking my right hand over the outside of his left arm.

Controlling Albert's head with my left arm, I chamber my right hand and prepare to throw an uppercut.

Pulling down on Albert's head with my left hand, I throw a right uppercut underneath his left arm.

Still maintaining control of Albert's head with my left arm, I chamber my right hand for another strike.

Bracing Albert's head with my left hand, I switch things up by throwing a right hook over his left arm.

BUMP THE ARM TO BACK

If you feel your opponent get lazy while pummeling in the clinch, you can sometimes take his back by bumping his arm upward, slipping underneath his arm, and then circling around behind him. If you're successful with this technique and manage to take your opponent's back, you've got multiple options. You can pick him up and slam him down or force him to the ground and secure back control, which I demonstrate in the next technique.

I'm tied up with Albert in the dirty boxing clinch.

I bring my right hand down, just as I did when preparing to unleash with an uppercut.

Instead of socking Albert with an uppercut, I blast my right arm straight up to clear his arm from my head. For the best results, you want to make contact just above your opponent's elbow.

As I blast my right arm upward to clear Albert's hand from my head, I turn my body in a counterclockwise direction.

As I continue to circle around Albert, I pull his head in a counterclockwise direction with my left hand.

Still pulling Albert's head in a counterclockwise direction with my left hand, I step my right foot behind him and hook my right arm over his back.

I secure my position by dropping my weight down on Albert's back and locking my arms tight around his body. To learn how to take your opponent's back from here, see the next technique.

BODY-LOCK TAKEDOWN TO BACK

In the previous technique I demonstrated one of several ways that you can move around to your opponent's back and secure a body-lock. When you accomplish this, utilizing this technique allows you to bring him to the ground and secure back control. The move is pretty basic. You simply wrap one of your legs around one of your opponent's legs, and then drive forward and collapse him to the ground. If your opponent applies backward pressure to avoid getting taken down, a good remedy is ease up on your forward pressure and just sit him down on his butt. Either way, you'll be in a good position to slap on the rear naked choke. The most important part of this move is squeezing your body-lock tight so your chest remains pinned to your opponent's back. If you lose this control, you won't get the takedown.

I've taken Albert's back and secured a body-lock.

Keeping my body-lock tight, I hook my left leg around Albert's left leg.

With my first hook established, I lean all my weight forward. It is important to note that sometimes your opponent will go down easy, and sometimes he will put up a fight. If he puts up a fight, you may need to hop around and maintain balance as you work him to the mat. Eventually your weight will wear on him and force him to the ground.

Pressing all my weight into Albert, his body is forced forward and he falls to the mat.

DIRTY BOXING CLINCH

Because I have Albert's left arm trapped underneath my left arm with my body-lock, he is unable to post on his left hand and automatically rolls onto his left shoulder.

Once I come down onto the ground, I pull Albert on top of me, roll toward my back, and work to hook my right leg around his right leg. If I can establish my second hook, I can secure back control.

I establish back control by hooking my right leg around Albert's right leg. As I do this, I prepare to slap on the rear naked choke by slipping my left arm around his neck.

To lock in the choke, I latch onto my right biceps with my left hand, and then I place my right hand behind Albert's head. Squeezing everything tight, I force Albert to tap.

THE STAND UP GAME

KNEE FROM FRONT HEADLOCK

Capturing an opponent in a front headlock while in the standing position gives you a lot of control. Your torso prevents your opponent from lifting his head, your under-hook prevents him from escaping out to the side, and your cup on his chin prevents him from backing out. It's a perfect opportunity to throw a couple of powerful knees. To set up a knee strike from the front headlock position, I like to push my opponent away to create some distance, and then use my grip on his head to rip him back into me as I throw the knee. After the knee lands, I rip him forward once again to make sure he remains off balance. Your opponent's only real option when caught in this position is to drop to his knees and go for the takedown, but because you're already in a good position to sprawl, his shot should be relatively easy to stuff. Once you've established sprawl control, you can drop more knees or circle around and take your opponent's back.

I'm tied up with Paco in the dirty boxing clinch.

To secure the front headlock position, I pull Paco's head down with my left hand and reach my right hand under his chin.

Positioning Paco's head in the center of my chest, I drop my weight down over his shoulders and grip the outside of his right arm with my left hand.

I step my right leg back.

As I fire my right knee straight forward, I pull Paco's head toward my knee to ensure he absorbs the entire impact of the knee.

After landing the knee, I bring my right leg back and then rip Paco forward to keep him off balance.

FIGHTING AGAINST THE CAGE

A good boxer understands how to use the ring to his advantage. He can trap his opponent in a corner, avoid getting trapped in the corner, and box while his back is against the ropes. To be a proficient mixed martial artist, you must learn how to fight in a steel cage.

Becoming a master at pinning your opponent's back against the cage increases your offensive options. When I back my opponent up against the fence, I usually go for a single- or double-leg takedown because I have robbed his ability to defend my takedown by sprawling. If you're a striker and want to keep the fight standing, pinning your opponent against the cage can create openings to land fierce elbow and knee strikes. The one thing you don't want to do when you achieve this advantageous position is become stagnant. No one likes to see two fighters hug each other and do nothing. If you rest too long, you not only give your opponent a chance to spin you around and drive you up against the fence, but you also risk having the referee break the fight apart due to inactivity.

Although it's more enjoyable to practice working from a position where you have the upper hand, it is mandatory that you learn how to defend yourself when your opponent manages to pin your back against the cage. You must know how to strike, spin your opponent around, and execute takedowns as your opponent drives his weight into you. When I'm pressed up against the cage, I make it very difficult for my opponent to take me down, but I've gotten points taken away on the judges' scorecards many times because I didn't utilize the tools in my arsenal to escape. Even though my opponent wasn't causing me any damage, he was the one pressing me up against the fence, and to the judges it appeared as though he was winning. So learn from my mistakes and stay active.

In the upcoming section I've included numerous techniques that you can utilize in both scenarios, but even more important than the techniques is developing cage sensitivity. This is something that can only come about with lots of practice and time. If you don't have a cage to train in, I recommend finding a sturdy wall.

Key Concepts for Pressing against the Cage

✓Maintain a low base and keep driving your weight into your opponent.
✓Maintain a staggered stance and keep your lead leg between your opponent's legs.
✓Whether you are working for a takedown or trying to keep the fight standing, stay active.

Key Concepts for Pinned against the Cage

✓Keep your hips at an angle. You never want your hips pinned flat against the cage.
✓Constantly work to reverse your position by creating distance or pivoting out. Every second you remain pinned against the cage, you're not only in danger of getting struck or taken down, but you're also allowing your opponent to rack up points on the judges' scorecards.

AVOIDING THE CAGE

One of the worst things that you can do in a fight is allow your opponent to press your back up against the cage. Although it is possible to work well from this position, making it very difficult for your opponent to take you down, you don't want to make a habit of fighting from here. The best way to avoid getting pinned up against the fence is to develop a good sense placement in the Octagon. At all times, you should know how far the fence is behind you. If your opponent begins driving you backward, you can utilize this technique to spin him around and turn the tables. To get comfortable with this technique, I recommend playing a sumo game where you and your training partner start out in the middle of the cage and then try to push each other back into the fence. Pay attention to your footwork, and use your opponent's footwork to force him off balance and spin him around as he drives into you.

I'm tied up with Albert in the clinch.

Albert drives me toward the cage, forcing me to step back with my left leg. Instead of stepping straight back, I step back towards my right side and begin turning my body in a counterclockwise direction. This will allow me to use Albert's linear momentum against him.

As Albert drives forward, I continue to turn in a counterclockwise direction.

As Albert continues to drive forward, I spin him around by pivoting in a counterclockwise direction on my left foot, pulling with my left under-hook, and pushing with my right over-hook.

I spin Albert all the way around so that his back is facing the cage.

Driving my weight forward, I pin Albert against the cage.

I finish by stepping my left leg between Albert's legs and driving my weight into him. For the best results, you want to pin your opponent's hips flat against the cage.

DOUBLE-LEG TAKEDOWN OFF THE CAGE

The moment I pin my opponent up against the cage, I'll immediately work for either the double- or single-leg take-down. I accomplish this by securing my base, wrapping up my opponent's legs, and then cutting the corner to take him down. If you're a striker and want to keep the fight standing, you should immediately begin setting up your strikes. It is very important to stay active when you get your opponent in this compromising position.

I've pinned Albert up against the cage. My feet are back, my base is low, and I'm driving my weight into Albert's midsection. I'm in a perfect position to work for the takedown.

Dropping down to my left knee, I wrap both arms around the back of Albert's legs and then push off my right leg. It's important to notice that I've kept my back straight and my head pressed into Albert's side.

Because I've secured Albert's legs, he has no choice but to fall to the mat as I drive my weight to my left side.

Keeping my weight pressed down into Albert to prevent him from scrambling, I avoid his legs and move right into side control.

CAGE TO SINGLE-LEG

A lot of the time when you pin an opponent up against the cage, he will position himself at an angle to prevent you from snatching up both of his legs. When I can't get the double due to the positioning of my opponent's hips, I immediately scoop up his nearest leg and work for the single.

I've pinned Reagan up against the cage. My feet are back, my base is low, and I'm driving my weight into Reagan's midsection. I'm in a perfect position to work for the takedown.

Keeping my weight pressed into Reagan, I bring my right hand between his legs and clasp my hands together behind his right thigh. From here I can begin working for the single-leg takedown.

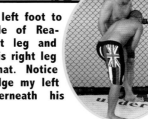

I step my left foot to the outside of Reagan's right leg and then lift his right leg off the mat. Notice how I wedge my left knee underneath his right leg.

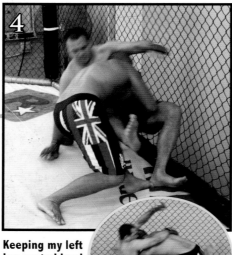

Keeping my left leg posted hard on the mat, I rotate in a counterclockwise direction and drive my weight and head into Reagan, forcing him to the ground.

I follow Reagan to the mat and establish the top position.

SINGLE TO DOUBLE-LEG TAKEDOWN

This technique comes in handy when you've secured your opponent's lead leg, but he has good balance and is defending the single. By walking his lead leg over to his rear leg, it allows you to lock your arms around both legs. It provides much better control because your opponent's legs are pinched together. It also eliminates his ability to scramble right back up to his feet the moment you take him down. Perhaps the most important thing to remember when you have your opponent up against the fence with his lead leg off the ground is to constantly work for the takedown. You see way too many fighters get the single and then just hold on. If you take your time, your opponent will most likely land some punches and pummel his arms in for an escape.

I've got Albert's left leg trapped and I'm working for a single-leg takedown.

Albert is doing an excellent job at maintaining balance, making the single-leg hard to manage. Instead of fighting him, I step my left leg forward and drive my weight into him. Notice how this pinches his legs together.

I wrap my right arm around Albert's right leg and grip my hands together.

I step my right foot forward.

I pull Albert's legs in, almost as if I were hiking a football between my legs. At the same time, I push my head forward to collapse his base.

Albert gets put onto his back.

FOOT STOMPS

Heel stomps are mainly designed to aggravate your opponent, but if one lands just right, you might get lucky and break his foot or toe or cause some type of damage that will hinder him later in the fight. They can also be used while pummeling for position as a distraction to set up another technique such as a takedown.

I've got Paco pinned up against the cage.

I lift my right foot.

I stomp my right heel onto the top of Paco's left foot. Notice how I arch my toes upward. This makes my heel as sharp as possible.

KNEEING AGAINST THE CAGE

Landing knees to your opponent's thighs or midsection while pressing him up against the cage usually won't end the fight, but they can wear him down over time and score you points on the judges' scorecards.

I've got Butch pinned up against the cage. Notice how I've positioned my left foot behind me.

Keeping Butch pinned against the cage with my left shoulder and hands, I drive a low left knee into his left thigh.

I return to my normal stance and reset my base.

After resetting my base, I mix things up by throwing my right knee at the exact same spot on Butch's left thigh.

I drop my right foot back and reset my base.

I execute a switch step, putting my left leg back. This creates the space I need to drive a straight left knee into Butch's midsection.

I drive a left knee straight into Butch's midsection. It is important to notice that my knee is going more forward than upward. This not only ensures a more damaging shot, but it also helps you maintain your balance.

I drop my left foot down and return to my normal stance.

PUMMELING FOR UNDER-HOOKS TO SWITCH COUNTER

When your opponent pins you up against the cage and begins working for a takedown, a good option is to turn your hips at an angle so they're not flat against the cage. This creates space between your opponent's body and your body, allowing you to pummel an arm in for an under-hook, lift your opponent's body away from your legs, spin him around, and trap him against the cage as I demonstrate below. Achieving these goals usually requires a battle, and the best way to avoid that battle is not to let your opponent pin you against the fence in the first place.

Troy has pinned me up against the cage. He is low on my hips, working for the takedown.

Immediately I work to get Troy off my legs. I begin by turning my hips in a clockwise direction. This creates space between Troy's body and my body, which allows me to pummel my right arm across the right side of his head and underneath his left arm.

Using my right under-hook, I lift Troy away from my legs. As I do this, I turn my hips in a counterclockwise direction so that I'm not pinned flat against the cage. From here I will work to pin Troy's back against the cage.

I step away from the cage with my right foot and then follow with my left. As I do this, I pivot on my left foot in a counterclockwise direction to turn Troy around. It is important to note that I'm pulling down on Troy's right arm with my left arm, and I'm driving my right under-hook upward.

Continuing to pivot in a counterclockwise direction, I begin driving my weight into Troy to pin him against the cage.

I pin Troy up against the cage.

THE STAND UP GAME

SINGLE-LEG COUNTER

When your hips are pinned flat against the cage and your opponent is working for the takedown, it's best to angle your hips, pummel in for an under-hook, and spin your opponent into the cage as you did in the previous technique. However, if your opponent has already dropped low for your legs, it can sometimes be difficult to pummel in and establish an under-hook. In such a case, this technique comes in very handy. Instead of working to under-hook your opponent's arm, you reach over his body and wrap your arms around his leg. As long as you execute the move with speed and proper form, you will be able to rip your opponent over to his back and obtain the top position.

Reagan has pinned me up against the cage. He is low on my hips, working for a takedown.

Reagan is super tight against my hips, making it difficult to pummel in for an under-hook. To avoid the takedown, I reach my left arm over his body and begin hooking it around the inside of his left leg.

I hook my left arm around the inside of Reagan's left leg and clasp my hands together.

Rotating my hips in a counterclockwise direction, I lift Reagan's left leg off the mat by curling my arms upward.

As I continue to drive my weight forward and rotate in a counterclockwise direction, Reagan crumbles to the mat.

I immediately drop my weight down on top of Reagan to prevent him from scrambling.

I wrap my left arm around the right side of Reagan's head, establishing the side control position.

STRIKING THE DOWNED GUARD

Striking at a downed opponent when you're standing is another situation completely unique to MMA competition. Usually you'll end up in this position when you knock your opponent down with a strike, execute a takedown or throw, or stand up in your opponent's guard. You may also end up here when fighting an opponent who wants to bring the fight to the ground but can't get the takedown, so he simply drops to his butt and scoots forward, trying to beckon you down.

You have many offensive options when in this position, and deciding which option to choose depends upon your goals in the fight. If you are primarily a striker, you may want to chop away at your opponent's legs with kicks, and then back away and let the referee stand the fight back up. If you're primarily a grappler like me, then you'll probably want to use the position to set up a pass. Passing can sometimes be difficult when fighting an experienced jiu-jitsu practitioner, so it usually helps to set your pass up with strikes. You will find several ways to accomplish this in the following pages.

One of the best things about striking at an opponent who is lying on his back is that you have a ton of creative leeway. If you've watched a fair share of MMA competitions, you know exactly what I mean. There are fighters who like flying stomp kicks, jumping over-hand punches, cartwheel passes, and all sorts of other strikes and passes that you never thought imaginable. Other than the up-kick, your opponent doesn't have much he can do in the way of strikes. However, just because you have a smaller chance of getting knocked out doesn't mean you should always try something crazy. It is still quite possible to lose your positioning, and in MMA position is everything. Before doing something that is considered risky, you need to factor in a lot of things. Are you winning the fight up to that point? How much time is left in the round? If your goal is to put on a show and you're confident in your ability to reverse any negative situation that could arise, you might want to make use of your creativity to add another clip to your highlight reel. But it is important to note that creativity is best used at a distance. Once you get into your opponent's guard, you must watch your base because your opponent has options.

Key Concepts for Striking the Downed Guard

✓Keep your head back and maintain good posture.
✓Keep your lead leg bent and strong.
✓If you gain control of your opponent's legs, immediately work to pass his guard, set up a strike, or both.

BASIC STANCE (ATTACKING THE DOWNED GUARD)

When striking at a downed opponent, one of the things you need to watch out for is the up-kick to the face. Gaining control of your opponent's legs by grabbing his ankles reduces his ability to land such a blow, but getting a hold of his ankles can be tricky. You never want to simply bend over and reach for them because you will most likely eat a heel to the chin. A better approach is to maintain the stance shown below and work to gain control of his legs. You want to bend your front leg slightly and keep it strong to hinder your opponent from being able to hyperextend your leg with a kick. You also want to lean back to keep your head and torso out of his foot's reach.

I keep my front leg bent and strong to prevent my opponent from being able to hyperextend my leg with a front kick to my knee. I lean my head back to avoid getting up-kicked in the face. I have my left arm out to guard against strikes, as well as to give me the ability to catch or gain control of my opponent's legs to set up a strike or pass.

STEPPING IN

If an opponent is lying defensively on his back in the shell position, it makes it relatively easy to close the distance and work to gain control. However, a lot of opponents lying on their back will machine-gun fire their legs, almost as if they are riding a bicycle. Trying to inch your way forward will usually result in eating a half a dozen kicks. In such a scenario, a good option is to lift your lead leg high and step between your opponent's legs. It requires precise timing to avoid getting struck, but once you manage your goal, your opponent can no longer kick your lead leg. Immediately you should lean your shin into his leg or body and work to gain control of his legs with your hands.

I'm standing a few feet away from Paco in my defensive posture, getting ready to close the distance and gain control of his legs.

Paco begins to machine gun his legs to keep me at bay. If I attempt to inch my way forward, I will get hammered with kicks. Instead, I need to close the distance in one step.

I lift my left leg high and push off of my right leg.

Keeping my head back to avoid getting nailed with an up-kick, I step my left leg between Paco's legs.

CONTROLLING THE LEGS

When your opponent is lying on his back and you're standing, it generally doesn't take that long for the referee to call a stop to the action and stand the fight back up. If you're a grappler who wants to keep the fight on the ground, you need to get in and make something happen. A good way to accomplish that is to step in and grab a hold of your opponent's ankles. Once you control his ankles, you have options. You can toss his legs to the side to set up a strike or pass, or you can use your ankle control to land a strike such as a face or belly stomp. Whatever option you decide to utilize, just do it quickly. You never want to pass up on a good opportunity to do some damage.

Keeping my head back, I reach down and grab Albert's ankles so that my thumbs are pointing upward. Ideally, you want to form your grip just above your opponent's heel on his achilles tendon.

THROWING LEGS TO OVERHAND

When an opponent is lying on his back and you manage to gain control of his ankles, a great option is to chuck his legs to one side or another and then dive forward with a powerful punch, passing his guard in the process. Although chucking the legs and punching works quite well, I like to spice it up a little by pretending to throw my opponent's legs to one side, and then quickly throwing them to the other. Because my opponent usually forces his legs in the opposite direction when I throw the fake, his resistance works against him when I change sides. In addition to helping clear my opponent's legs out of the way, the fake also loads up my right hand, which allows me to drop the punch down with some serious authority. However, every halfway decent jiu-jitsu practitioner knows he is in danger the moment you secure his legs, and he will most likely fight to free his legs and regain the guard position. For this reason, it is important that you execute this technique the moment you gain control of his ankles.

Having gained control of Paco's legs, I'm ready to set up my attack.

I fake throwing Paco's legs to my left, making him think I will pass on my right.

Quickly throwing Paco's legs to the right, I cock my right hand back and prepare to deliver an overhand to his face. Notice how tossing Paco's legs has primed me for the overhand, just like a left hook primes my hips for a right cross.

As Paco is forced onto his side, I drop my left hand to clear his right arm away from the path of my punch.

Snapping my hips in a counterclockwise direction as I come down, I drop a ruthless overhand right to Paco's face. It's important to notice that I'm dropping my weight down and really putting the force of my body into the punch. Not only does this allow me to hit harder, but it also leads me right into the pass.

Dropping all the way to the mat, I wrap Paco up and establish side control.

ANKLE LOCK DEFENSE

When your opponent is lying on his back and you're standing directly above him, you have to constantly be on the lookout for getting caught in an ankle lock. It's pretty much the only submission your opponent can manage from his compromised position, but it's a pretty easy submission for him to slap on, especially when you attack with a belly or face stomp. It's much like arm bars in that if you just stand there and let your opponent slowly synch in the ankle lock, you're not going to be able to get out. The instant he wraps his leg around your leg, you must peel his leg off you and then come down into him, most likely falling into his half guard. As I come down, I like to make my opponent pay by throwing a powerful overhand. The best way to avoid the whole scenario is to gain control of your opponent's legs and quickly pass his guard.

1. I'm hovering over Paco, searching for an opening to attack.

2. Going for an ankle lock, Paco swings his right leg between my legs.

3. Continuing to set up the ankle lock, Paco hooks his right leg over my left leg.

4. In order to prevent getting caught in an ankle lock, I need to unhook Paco's right leg from my left leg. To begin this process, I reach my left hand around Paco's right foot and cup his heel in my palm.

5. I pull Paco's right leg to the outside of my hips using my left hand. As I do this, I prepare to drop a savage overhand to his face.

6. Still holding Paco's right leg at bay with my left hand, I come down with the punch.

7. Using my downward momentum, I land a devastating overhand to Paco's jaw.

8. I finish by dropping all the way down into Paco's half guard.

BELLY STOMP

Gaining control of a downed opponent's legs opens up an assortment of stomps. The stomp to the face is always a good option, but it has been outlawed in MMA competition in America for quite some time. If you're competing in the United States, a stomp to the belly is a good alternative.

I've gained control of Paco's legs, putting me in a good position to attack.

Keeping Paco's legs split apart using my hands, I lift my right knee.

I drive my right heel down into Paco's belly.

Without wasting any time, I pull my right leg back and return to my normal stance. It is important to note that when executing this move you will be vulnerable to getting caught in an ankle lock so you should get in and out as quickly as possible. If you can knock the wind out of your opponent, it will make it easier to execute strikes or a pass.

FACE STOMP

The Face Stomp can cause quite a bit of damage to your opponent, but because the technique requires that you extend your leg so far forward, it can also put you in a vulnerable spot when done with improper technique. If your opponent is a leg lock specialist, the chances are he will attempt to secure your leg after you land the stomp to prevent you from pulling it free. To get the leverage you need to quickly retract your leg, you must turn your body away from your opponent after landing the strike and then push off of his face with your foot.

I've gained control of Paco's legs, putting me in a good position to attack.

Still controlling Paco's legs, I lift my right knee.

Driving my hips forward and extending my right leg, I stomp my heel into Paco's face.

To prevent getting caught in an ankle lock, I quickly turn my body in a counterclockwise direction.

Having turned my body around, I smear my right foot into Paco's face and push off. This step is very important because reaching so far forward with the face stomp really extends your body, and the push off gives you that extra boost to get your leg out of there in a hurry. It will also help you free your leg if your opponent should quickly latch onto it.

I pull my right leg free, escaping any potential leg locks.

I return to my stance and search for another opening to attack.

PUNCH TO PASS

This is another option for when you gain control of a downed opponent's legs. Instead of using your control to stomp him in the belly or face, you use your control to force his legs back toward his head and put him up onto his shoulders. Digging your hips underneath his back keeps him trapped on his shoulders and allows you to get your offense going. His head will be lying on the mat beneath you, so punching him in the face is always a good option. Sakuraba, a well known Japanese MMA fighter, likes to keep his opponents trapped in this position for a prolonged period of time and just punch away. I personally like to sock my opponent a couple of times, and then transition to side control so I can start working for the mount or back.

I'm hovering over Paco, searching for an opening to attack.

In one movement, I drop my level, gain control of Paco's legs, and drive forward by pushing off my right leg.

Using my arms, I drive Paco's legs toward his head. Notice how this elevates his hips off the mat.

As soon as Paco's hips rise off the mat, I fall to my right knee and position my hips underneath his hips. This limits his mobility, giving me an opportunity to strike or pass his guard. It is important to notice that I am posting on my left leg. This increases my balance and mobility, which will help me achieve my attack.

As I load up my right hand, I place my left hand on Paco's right hip to further control his body.

I drop my right hand between Paco's legs and smash it into his face. Notice how throwing the punch has turned my hips. This sets me up to pass on my right side.

Immediately I bring my right hand to the outside of Paco's left leg. At the same time, I rotate my hips and shoulders in a counterclockwise direction, which steers Paco over onto his right shoulder. It is important to notice that I've kept my hips pressed tightly against Paco. You don't want to give up too much space during the transition because it will cause you to lose control.

Pressing my weight into Paco, I drive my right arm across his neck. This forces him to roll further over onto his right shoulder.

As Paco comes down onto his right side, I press my weight down on top of him.

I drop my left leg back and force Paco to his back using my weight and right arm.

Dropping my hips to the mat, I secure the side control position by pinning Paco on his back using my weight.

PUNT KICK TO FACE

A lot of times when you're standing over a downed opponent, he will prop himself up on one elbow and hold his other arm out to defend against strikes. In such a situation, I will sometimes grab a hold of his outstretched hand. This not only hinders his ability to block with that arm, but it also distracts him. Then I will throw a roundhouse kick at his head. Even if your opponent manages to free the arm you're holding onto, he usually won't be able to block the entire force of your kick.

I'm standing above Reagan, staying close to prevent him from making a quick escape to his feet.

I reach out and grab a hold of Reagan's left hand. This is partially to distract him from my upcoming kick, and partially to prevent him from using his arm to block my kick. If I can take his left arm out of the picture, his only way to block the kick will be to drop to his back.

With Reagan still wondering why I latched onto his hand, I throw a left kick to the right side of his face.

KICKING UNDER THE LEG

Whenever your opponent is on his back and you're standing above him, it's never hurts to land a couple of kicks underneath his leg. Not only does it look good to the judges, but it can also hinder your opponent's movement later in the fight. The technique works best when you have control of your opponent's legs because it prevents him from blocking your strike by balling up the shell.

I'm controlling Albert's left leg with my right hand.

Using my right hand to lift Albert's left leg upward, I drive in a right low kick to his thigh.

I quickly return to my previous stance and search for another opening.

Part Two
THE GROUND GAME

FIGHTING FROM THE DOWNED GUARD

There are many ways that you can end up on your back while your opponent is standing. You could get knocked down with a punch or kick. Your opponent could trip you or stand up in your guard. However you end up in this terrible spot, your main goal should be to escape back to your feet. This is often difficult to manage when your opponent is standing within striking range because he can land a kick to your head or haul you back to the mat the moment you begin to rise. To safely get up, you need to create separation between you and your opponent. One way to accomplish this is to throw up-kicks at his legs, body, and head. If you can create distance and make your opponent fearful of coming forward or down with an attack, standing up becomes a whole lot easier. You should take this option whenever possible, even if you want the fight to remain on the ground. As I have already mentioned, MMA is not just a grappling match. Even the best jiu-jitsu practitioners in the world are susceptible to getting knocked out with a stomp kick to the head or a heavy, downward punch from the downed guard. A better approach is to get up, set up a takedown, and secure the top position.

If your opponent manages to move close enough to where he is standing between your legs, your options change. You might still be able to land an up-kick to his face, but there are better options available. I like to use both the Goes and De La Riva guard positions. Not only do these positions make it difficult for your opponent to gain control of your legs and strike, but they also allow you to counter your opponent's available strikes, opening numerous options in the process. These options include getting back to your feet, sweeping your opponent over to his back, and pulling him down into your guard. Although sweeping your opponent or escaping back to your feet is more desirable than pulling him into your guard, you sometimes have to take what you can get. As a result, it is important that you drill each of the techniques I have included in the upcoming section so you'll be prepared to deal with a variety of scenarios.

Key Concepts for Fighting from the Downed Guard
✓Transitioning to the shell allows you to defend kicks and throw kicks of your own.
✓Get up whenever the opportunity presents itself. Timing and sense of distance is everything.
✓Never let your opponent gain control of your legs.

THE SHELL

When you're lying on your back and your opponent is standing, there are three ranges of combat. The first range is where your opponent is maintaining enough distance so that he can't strike you and you can't strike him. I refer to this as the "get-up range" because it is an ideal time to escape back to your feet. The second range is where your opponent is standing between your legs in your open guard. When you find yourself in this position, you want to utilize the De La Riva and Goes guards to neutralize your opponent's attacks and either get up to your feet, sweep your opponent to his back, or pull him down into your guard. The third range is where your opponent is standing just far enough away that he can land strikes. In this range, you want to utilize the shell. Keeping your hands up allows you to protect your face from punches. Keeping your knees lifted up to your elbows helps protect the lower half of your body from kicks, as well as gives you the option of launching kicks of your own to force your opponent back into the "get-up range." If you're in the shell and your opponent attempts to walk around you to create an opening to attack, you want to spin with him by rocking your body back and forth. To be effective in the shell, you must keep your opponent in front of your legs.

Lying on my back, I bring my knees up to my elbows to create a solid barrier on both sides of my body. From this position, I can kick or snap up to my feet on a moment's notice.

BLOCKING A KICK FROM THE SHELL

If you're lying on your back and your opponent throws a kick, you want to assume the shell position to minimize the damage. Of course you don't just want to ball up in the shell and let your opponent land one kick after another. You want to machine-gun your legs into your opponent's legs, torso, or face. At the very least you will force him back out of striking range, which allows you to work back to your feet.

I'm lying on my back. Paco is standing before me, searching for an opening to attack.

As Paco throws a right roundhouse kick at my left leg, I bring my knees up to my elbows to create a solid barrier. Having assumed the shell position, his kick bounces off my shin.

GETTING UP

If you manage to force your opponent outside of striking range or he willingly gives you that distance, you want to explode back to your feet utilizing this technique. It's something that most jiu-jitsu practitioners learn on their first day, yet it is the most overlooked move of all time. It's pretty self-explanatory. First, prop yourself up on one arm. Watch your opponent's footwork and search for an opening to explode back to your feet. If your opponent comes in with a kick as you're on your way up, drop back into the shell and immediately start throwing push kicks to create distance. What you don't want is to get up slow and allow your opponent to hone in on his target and throw a fight-ending strike. You have to drill this movement over and over so you can explode up in a flash. Anytime you're lying down at the beach, chilling on the mats, or watching TV on your living room floor, you want to utilize this technique to get up. In a few weeks time you will realize that it's the most natural and effective way to get up off your back.

I'm lying on my back in the shell.

Seeing that I have the distance I need to escape up to my feet, I turn to my right side, post up on my right elbow, drop my right leg to the ground, and coil my left leg in. I keep my left arm straight out to gauge distance and protect my face.

To get my hips off the mat, I come up onto my right hand and push off the ground with my left foot.

As I pull my right leg back and plant my right foot, I keep my left arm extended for safety.

Standing all the way up, I assume my standard fighting stance.

DROPPING UNDER A KICK

As I have already mentioned, it is important to execute proper timing when exploding up to your feet. The first step is to prop yourself up on one hand. Although this prevents you from being able to use your posted arm to block your opponent's strikes, it gets you that much closer to your feet. It also increases your elevation, so if your opponent throws a kick at your head, you can simply drop down to your elbow, make your opponent miss, and then use his compromised positioning to explode up to the standing position.

Seeing that I have the necessary distance I need to escape up to my feet, I post on my right hand and left foot and prepare to lift my hips off the mat.

Beach steps his right foot forward and throws a left roundhouse kick at my head. As he does this, I drop down to my elbow. This lowers my level and allows the kick to whiz by my head. Notice that in addition to getting my head out of the way, I have also cleared my left arm from the kick's path. The reason I haven't dropped all the way down to my back is because I still want to escape to my feet. If I can make Beach completely miss the kick, I will have the opportunity to do that as long as I'm on my elbow.

Having missed the kick, Beach loses balance and plants his right foot outside of his normal fighting stance. This exposes his back and creates an opening to use the previous technique to get back to my feet.

STOMP KICK TO THE LEG

Although the shell is primarily a defensive position, you still have a few strikes in your arsenal. The stomp kick to your opponent's lead leg is perhaps the most practical one. You want to drive your foot powerfully forward, striking just above your opponent's kneecap. Even if your opponent has his front leg bent, this strike can be quite a nuisance and force him to back off, which often creates an opening to snap back to your feet. If your opponent makes the mistake of keeping his front leg straight, then a hard stomp kick to his leg can hyperextend his knee and fold him forward. But no matter how proficient you are at stomp kicks, you don't want to get comfortable fighting from this position. As long as your opponent is standing and you're on your back, he will have a lot more options in the offense department. You want to use the strikes in your arsenal to help you get back to your feet.

With Paco hovering above me in striking range, I've assumed the shell position.

I throw a straight right stomp kick, landing just above Paco's left kneecap. My goal is to buckle him forward and hyperextend his knee. At the very least, the strike will make him think twice about coming in.

SPRING STOMP KICK

Renzo Gracie kept trying this move when we fought in the K-1 World Grand Prix in Hawaii. Although I won the fight, this technique got under my skin, and I thought, "Now I've got to use it on someone else." To execute this move from the shell, you want to hold your knees tightly with your arms, while at the same time applying outward pressure with your legs. When you let go of your knees, your legs spring out extremely fast. It's a deceptive and effective technique to utilize when you're lying on your back and your opponent is coming forward, looking to gain control of your legs.

Instead of assuming the shell position, I grab a hold of my shins with my hands and pull my legs into my body. At the same time, I apply outward pressure with both of my legs. The idea is to create a loaded spring with your legs so that when you release them, they explode toward your opponent.

I let go of my right leg. This releases the built up tension and snaps my right leg forward. The kick lands just above Paco's left knee, buckling his leg and folding his body forward.

LEFT UP-KICK FROM SHELL

Another attack at your disposal when balled up in the shell is the up-kick, and it can pay off to utilize it whenever the opportunity presents itself. It is the holy grail of kicks when you're on the bottom. If you get your heel involved and land flush, there is a good possibility that you'll get the knockout. At the very least, you will make your opponent think twice before coming in, which will usually give you the space needed to snap back up to your feet. The key to success with this technique is using your elbows to push your hips off the ground while thrusting your leg upward. For obvious reasons, timing is also of the essence.

Paco makes the mistake of leaving his head down while closing the distance.

Posting on my elbows and pushing off, I elevate my hips and thrust my left foot into Paco's unprotected face.

HEEL STOMP FROM SHELL

As you move your legs around to hinder your opponent from gaining control of them, this is a good technique to pull out of your bag of tricks. It certainly won't end the fight, but it can irritate your opponent and make him think twice about battling for leg control.

With Paco hovering above me in striking range, I assume the shell position and plant my right foot on his left thigh.

Pushing my right foot off Paco's thigh, I raise my hips off the ground, roll back onto my shoulders, and bring my left leg straight up.

Generating downward momentum by dropping my hips to the mat, I snap my left heel down into Paco's thigh. Notice how I flex my foot back to make my heel as sharp as possible.

BREAKING GRIPS TO PUSH KICK

When you're lying on your back and your opponent is standing, you never want to let him gain control of your legs because he can set up a strike or pass. To prevent this from happening, you want to constantly be moving your legs away from your opponent, into your opponent, and from side to side. If your opponent latches on to a leg, you want to break his grip by moving your leg away from his palm toward the opening of his hand, which is the weakest part of his grip due to the gap between his thumb and fingers. Once you break his grip, a good option is to kick your opponent away to create the room you need to stand back up. If you become a master at preventing your opponent from gaining control of your legs, most of the time he will either back away or jump into your guard.

I'm on my back with Paco above me. Having gained control of my legs, he is preparing to attack.

Before Paco has a chance to throw my legs to the side, I move my right leg toward the opening of his hand to break his grip. I then swing my right leg around his left arm in a counterclockwise direction.

Thrusting my hips out, I place my right foot on his midsection and force him backwards with a push kick.

Having freed my legs from Paco's grasp, I will now work on getting back to my feet.

BREAKING GRIPS TO DE LA RIVA

When an opponent gains control of your legs, the first thing you must do is break his grips. Once that is accomplished, you have a couple of different options. You can force him away as I did in the previous technique using a push kick or you can wrap a leg around his lead leg and assume the De La Riva guard position. The latter isn't as good as escaping back to your feet, but escaping to your feet can often be hard to manage. It's always good to have options. The De La Riva guard gives you control of your opponent's lead leg, which allows you to move him around and disrupt his balance as he tries to set up his attacks. It works hand and hand with the Goes guard, and switching back and forth between the two increases the range in which you are effective. If you are already familiar with the De La Riva guard from jiu-jitsu, you have a major leg up, but you still need to figure out which techniques work against an opponent who is trying to strike.

I'm on my back with Mark hovering above me. He has gained control of my legs, putting him in a good position to attack. Deciding to transition into the De La Riva guard position, I latch onto his left ankle with my right hand.	Driving my left foot into Mark's left hip, I pull my right leg toward the opening of his hand to break his grip.	I circle my right foot in a clockwise direction around Mark's left hand.	I achieve the De La Riva position by wrapping my right leg around Mark's left leg and hooking my right foot on the inside of his thigh.

UP-KICK FROM DE LA RIVA

When you're in the De La Riva position and your opponent throws an overhand, you have several options. The first option is to use the foot you have planted on his hip to halt his downward progression, which hinders him from landing the overhand. Another option is to remove your foot from his hip the moment you see him wind up for the punch. As his weight starts to drop, you throw a powerful up-kick into his face.

I've got Beach secured in the De La Riva guard position.	Beach draws back his right hand so he can drop down into my guard and deliver a powerful overhand to my face. The moment he does this, I remove my left foot from his hip and chamber my leg.	As Beach drops down to deliver the overhand, I launch my left foot into his face.

OVERHAND RIGHT COUNTER TO DE LA RIVA SWEEP

When I'm in the De La Riva position and my opponent drops in with a big overhand punch, there are three options that I utilize. With jiu-jitsu being my specialty, I usually prefer this option because it not only allows me to bring the fight to the ground, but it also puts me in the top position. As my opponent throws the overhand, I'll make a shell with my knee and elbow on the side of my body the punch is heading toward, and then collapse my legs and pull him into me. Due to this action and the fact that the overhand requires serious commitment, my opponent loses balance and comes down on top of me. From there, I utilize the De La Riva guard to sweep him over to his back.

I've assumed the De La Riva guard position by wrapping my right leg all the way around Paco's left leg, hooking my right foot around his inner left thigh, placing my left foot on his left hip to maintain distance, and latching onto his left ankle with my right hand for control.

In order to close the distance between us and land an overhand right, Paco pulls my left leg away from his body using his left hand.

The instant Paco pulls my left leg away from his body, I draw my left knee toward my head and to the inside of my left elbow. This creates a barrier on the left side of my body that protects me from the overhand. In addition to this, I also lift my left arm above my head to catch the punch early in its descent.

As Paco throws the overhand, his momentum carries his weight forward and down. I help aid this progression by balling up and drawing his body into me using my right De La Riva hook. It is important to notice how I wrap my left arm around Paco's head to control his posture. This will help me sweep him over.

Instead of wrapping both of my legs around Paco's waist and pulling full guard, I plant my left foot on his right hip.

I drive Paco's body over and to my right using my right De La Riva hook. As I do this, I push off his right hip with my left foot. Notice how these combined actions lift his right leg off the mat and starts turning his lower body over.

Still with my knees up toward my chest, I continue to sweep Paco over using my legs. It is important to notice that by straightening my right leg, I trap Paco's right leg and hindering him from bringing it back down to the mat. It is also important to notice that I'm still using my left arm to prevent him from posturing up.

I successfully sweep Paco over to my right side, putting him on his back.

As Paco comes down to his back, I pull on his head with my left hand to help me up to my knees. Once there, I establish the top position.

OVERHAND RIGHT COUNTER TO STANDING

If you attempt the previous sweep from the De La Riva guard position and your opponent counters by basing out on his far leg, you can use his compromised position to escape back to your feet as demonstrated below.

I've assumed the De La Riva guard position by wrapping my right leg all the way around Paco's left leg, hooking my right foot around his inner left thigh, placing my left foot on his left hip to maintain distance, and latching onto his left ankle with my right hand for control.

In an effort to close the distance and land an overhand right, Paco latches onto my left foot and tries to move it to his left side.

The instant Paco grabs a hold of my foot, I retract my left leg and bring my knee to the inside of my left elbow. This creates a barrier and prevents his overhand from landing. It is important to notice that I've held my left arm up to catch the punch early in its descent.

While Paco's weight is still moving forward with the punch, I place my left foot on his right hip, wrap my left arm around the back of his head to control his posture, and I draw my right leg into me. Because I have his left leg hooked with my right leg, it brings his weight forward even more.

5 Keeping Paco's left leg trapped with my De La Riva hook, I drive his right hip upward using my left foot. As Paco's body gets elevated, I control his posture using my left arm and begin sweeping him over to my right side.

6 As I attempt to sweep Paco over, he manages to post his right leg. Although the sweep failed, I immediately decide to use the space generated by the sweep to get up to my feet.

7 I sit up and post on my right hand.

8 Posting my left foot on the mat, I unhook my right leg and post it on the mat behind me. Keeping my left hand on Paco's head allows me to gauge distance.

9 I stand all the way up and begin plotting my next attack.

DE LA RIVA TO GUARD

In order to sweep your opponent from the De La Riva guard when he throws an overhand punch, you must pull him forward with your hook to get his weight on top of you. If you can't get his weight far enough forward to execute the sweep, a good option is to pull full guard.

I've assumed the De La Riva guard position by wrapping my right leg all the way around Paco's left leg, placing my left foot on his left hip to maintain distance, and latching onto his left ankle with my right hand for control.

Paco attempts to land a left overhand punch, but because I keep my right leg straight and my left foot planted on his left hip, he is unable to close the distance.

Having failed to land the left overhand, Paco loads up to throw a right overhand punch.

Paco comes down with his right hand. To block his punch, I ball up by bringing my left leg to the inside of my left elbow. This creates a shield on the left side of my body.

DE LA RIVA GUARD

As Paco throws the overhand, his momentum carries his weight forward and down. I help aid this progression by balling up and drawing his body into me using my right De La Riva hook. It is important to notice that I have wrapped my left arm around his head for control, and that I'm still gripping his left ankle with my right hand.

Unable to get Paco's weight over the top of me, I abandon the sweep. As he collapses forward, I wrap both legs around his body to capture him in my full guard.

I bring my right ankle over my left and interlock my feet, establishing the closed guard position. I keep my arms wrapped tightly around Paco's head to keep his posture broken. This not only helps protect me from strikes, but it will also help me set up a submission or sweep.

GETTING UP FROM DE LA RIVA

When in the De La Riva position, using this technique is a good way to create distance between you and your opponent so you can escape back to your feet. If your right leg is wrapped around your opponent's left leg, then you punch your right foot all the way between your opponent's legs and hook it around your opponent's far hip. Once you have that positioning established, pushing on your opponent's hip with your foot turns his body and exposes his back. With your opponent's body turned, you plant your opposite foot on his side and kick him away. Because your opponent now has to turn back around before he can close the distance you created, it gives you a window of opportunity to snap back up to your feet.

I've assumed the De La Riva guard position by wrapping my right leg all the way around Beach's left leg, hooking my right foot around his left thigh, placing my left foot on his left hip to maintain distance, and latching onto his left ankle with my right hand for control.

Pushing off Beach's left hip with my left foot, I roll onto my right shoulder and get my hips off the mat.

Rolling all the way onto my right shoulder, I drive my right foot into Beach's right thigh by straightening my leg. Notice how this turns his body in a clockwise direction and exposes his back.

Letting go of Beach's ankle, I straighten my right leg completely. As this pressure turns him in a clockwise direction and exposes his back, I plant my left foot on his buttocks.

DE LA RIVA GUARD

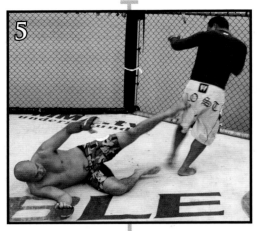

Driving my left foot into Beach's butt as hard as I can, I force him away from me. Before Beach can close the distance I created, he needs to turn around. This will buy me enough time to escape up to my feet.

Posting my right hand and left foot on the mat, I begin working back to my feet.

I climb to my feet and assume my fighting stance.

DE LA RIVA TO GOES GUARD

In the photos below I'm demonstrating how the De La Riva and Goes guards work interchangeably. Although both are highly effective in MMA competition, you have different options from each. In some situations it will be beneficial to assume the De La Riva guard, and in some situations the Goes guard will be more beneficial. Understanding how to switch back and forth between them is a must when you need to make something happen.

I've assumed the De La Riva guard position by wrapping my right leg all the way around Tony's left leg, hooking my right foot around his inner left thigh, placing my left foot on his left hip to maintain distance, and latching onto his left ankle with my right hand for control.	I unravel my right leg from around Tony's left leg. I then remove my left foot from his left hip, but immediately place my right foot on his left hip.	I lower my left leg and hook my foot around the back of Tony's right knee, establishing the Goes guard.

GOES GUARD PUSH SWEEP

This is the first technique I will attempt when I establish the Goes guard position because it's right there for the taking and doesn't require much movement. If this technique doesn't work because my opponent pushes my foot off his hip or steps back with his far leg, then I will execute the Goes switch sweep. It is important to note that the Goes guard is not a position that you can hold for a prolonged period of time, so make your move quickly.

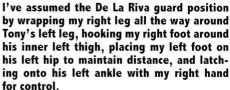

I've secure the Goes guard by planting my right foot on Mark's left hip, gripping his left ankle with my right hand, and hooking my left foot around the back of his right leg.	To sweep Mark to his back, I do three things at once. I extend my right leg to force his body backwards, I collapse his right knee by drawing my left hook towards my body, and I tug his left leg toward my head using my right hand. With this last movement, cupping your opponent's heel with your hand offers the best control.	My combined actions force Mark to fall to his back.	Sitting up, I get to my knees and establish the top position.

GOES GUARD SWITCH SWEEP

When you establish the Goes Guard, utilizing the Goes guard push sweep is an excellent option. However, if your opponent throws your foot off his hip or steps back with his far leg, causing you to lose the hook you have behind his knee, you want to immediately transition to the Goes guard switch sweep, which is the technique I show here.

I've secured the Goes guard by planting my right foot on Mark's left hip, gripping his left ankle with my right hand, and hooking my left foot around the back of his right leg.

Mark pushes my right foot off of his hip so he can drop down with an overhand right. The moment he does this, I unhook my left foot from behind his right leg.

I kick my left foot into Mark's left hip. This prevents him from closing the distance and dropping down with the punch. As I do this, I maneuver my right leg in-between Mark's legs.

Still driving my left foot into Mark's left hip, I chop my right foot into the back of his right leg to take it out from underneath him. At the same time, I pull his left ankle toward my head. It is important that you maintain pressure with your left leg so your opponent falls backwards instead of forward into your guard.

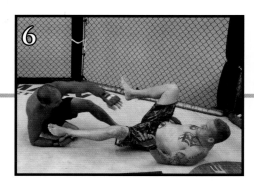

Mark has no choice but to fall to his back.

Immediately I begin to sit up.

Sitting all the way up, I roll onto my right knee and post on my left foot. Having claimed the top position, I'm ready to attack.

GUARD TOP

Every time you step into the cage, your job is to finish the fight. If you find yourself in the top guard position, the chances are you got there by either setting up a takedown off strikes or countering one of your opponent's strikes with a takedown. The point is that you most likely had to go through a battle to obtain the position, so make something happen. If you just sit there with your head buried in your opponent's chest, you not only tell the judges that you have no desire to finish the fight, but you also run the risk of having the referee stand the fight back up, which means you have to battle for the takedown all over again.

When I obtain the top guard position, my ultimate goal is to obtain the mount or take my opponent's back because they are both excellent positions from which to finish the fight with strikes or a submission. The first step to reaching either destination is to pass my opponent's guard, and the only way I can achieve that is by forcing him to open his legs. I'll generally do this by bombing on him with strikes. I'm not talking about throwing the occasional blow; I'm talking about unloading with overhands, uppercuts, hammer fists, and elbows. This initial blast will either knock my opponent out or force him to defend against my strikes by opening his guard and getting his legs involved. As he opens his guard, his focus is still on defending against strikes, so it allows me to set up a pass. If my opponent quickly shifts gears and begins defending the pass, it steals his focus away from strikes and allows me to land hard, clean punches. Those clean punches will either knock him out or put his focus back onto defending against strikes, which in turn allows me to set up another pass. Constantly switching back and forth and mixing these two modes together not only increases your chances of landing some hard shots, but it also increases your chance of executing a successful pass.

I'm not saying that you have to turn every fight into a grappling match. Concentrating exclusively on strikes while in the top guard can win a fight so long as each strike you throw gets you closer to the knockout. However, you must be prepared to deal with your opponent's reactions to those strikes. Unless you knock him out, he won't lie there and let you beat on him. He will employ movement, and if all you're thinking about is strikes, you're not only going to miss a prime opportunity to pass into a more dominant position, but your opponent might also escape from the bottom guard position. The bottom line is you must understand how strikes and grappling work together when on the ground, even if you don't always choose to blend them together. If you have to switch modes, you're going to miss out on opportunities and put yourself at risk of getting caught.

Key Concepts for Guard Top

✓ Stay active. Use your strikes to set up passes, and use your passes to set up strikes.
✓ Never put your hands on the mat.
✓ Maintain control positions whenever you're postured up or pinning your opponent to the mat.
✓ Always work to establish a more dominant position such as side control, mount, or back by passing.

POSTURE UP GUARD

Some fighters prefer to strike and set up passes while postured up in their opponent's guard, and others prefer to strike and set up passes while postured down. It all depends on the fighter and his personal preference. In my opinion, working from the postured up position is the best option because not only do you have a good base to work with, but you can also come down with the full authority of your weight. And unless your opponent sits up, you're in no danger of getting swept or submitted. Below I show the basic positioning of the postured up guard, and later in this section I will show how to set up strikes with passes and passes with strikes from this position.

I'm postured up in Beach's guard. Posting my left hand on his chest, I straighten my left arm to prevent him from sitting up into me. Keeping my right hand back allows me to pry his legs apart or throw a powerful punch at his face. To avoid being swept, I keep my back straight and maintain a solid base.

BICEPS CONTROL

You never want to place your hands on the mat because your opponent can lock your arm down with an over-hook and start to set up submissions. By pinning your opponent's arms to the mat with your hands, you not only nullify his set-ups, but you can also begin working to pass his guard. As you create movement and work to make something happen, you will transition back and forth between this position and the regular postured up position.

Cupping my hands over Mark's biceps, I straighten my arms to pin his arms to the mat. Notice that instead of wrapping my thumbs underneath his arms, I have placed them on top of his biceps.

FRIENDSHIP POSITION

It can sometimes be difficult to open your opponent's legs when he has them locked tightly around you. If your goal is to pass his guard, you must sometimes get creative. What I like to do is come up onto my feet, stack my opponent by driving my head down into his face, and work a little ground and pound. It is a very uncomfortable position for your opponent to be in, and if you manage to land some good strikes, he will most likely try to create separation between your bodies by opening his guard, placing his feet on your hips, and pushing you away. The moment he uncrosses his legs, you have a window of opportunity to stand-up all the way and gain control of his legs or utilize any of the pass sequences in this book.

I'm sitting in Beach's guard, pinning both of his arms to the mat.

Leaning my weight forward, I place my head underneath Beach's chin.

Coming up onto both feet, I drive my weight forward into Beach's face.

Elevating my hips, I drive all my weight forward into Beach's face. This causes him an ample amount of discomfort. If he reacts by opening his legs, I'm either going to return to my former positioning and reestablish my base, sit down with one knee elevated, or back out and work to pass his guard. Deciding which option to choose depends upon your goals in the fight.

BODY-BODY-HEAD

This punching combination is the bread and butter of ground and pound. If you listen closely to a couple of MMA fights that end up in the guard position, you're bound to hear a corner man shout "body-body-head' to the guy on top. The reason this combination works so well is because your opponent is forced to block the body shot, and the moment he does this, it creates an opening to land a punch to his face. It is important that you develop other combinations that fit well with your style, but this one must be practiced and perfected. The first two punches to the body are basically set-up shots, the equivalent to the standing jab, and the punch to the face is the power blow.

   The one thing you must always pay attention to when utilizing this combination is the arm you're not punching with. A lot of fighters get so consumed with beating on their opponent's body with one hand, they forget all about the other. As a result, they end up getting caught in an arm bar. To avoid this outcome, you must pay attention to your opponent's hips. If he starts opening his legs or working for the arm bar, you need to posture up and look to pass.

I'm in Reagan's full guard.

Reagan has his left hand hooked around the back of my head to control my posture, leaving the left side of his body open for punches. I cock my right hand back to throw a body hook to his ribs.

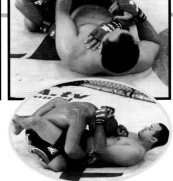

I drive my right fist into Reagan's rib cage.

I cock my right fist back to throw another body hook to Reagan's ribs.

Reagan starts dropping his elbow to block the body hook, but I manage to sneak past his defense and land another shot to his ribs.

Instead of throwing another punch to Reagan's ribs, which are now protected by his elbow, I throw an over-the-top punch towards his jaw. It is important to remember that this string of punches is done in rapid succession. If your opponent doesn't drop his elbow to protect his body after the second punch, just keep hitting his ribs until he does. When he finally reacts, go upstairs to his face.

My right hand crashes into Reagan's jaw.

OVER-THE-TOP-ELBOW

A lot of opponents will instinctively grab a hold of your wrists when you're in their guard to set up submissions and prevent you from punching them in the face. When your opponent decides to play wrist control, a good option is to fold your arm over his arm and land an elbow to his face. Your opponent will probably attempt to lift his arm to protect his face, but as long as you fold your elbow all the way over his arm, the strike will usually land flush.

I'm in Mark's full guard. He's controlling my wrists with his hands, trying to hinder me from punching.

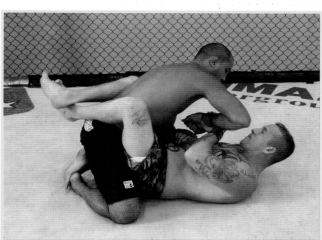

Unable to punch due to Mark's wrist control, I decide to throw an over the top elbow. I begin by leaning slightly to my left and rotating my right shoulder up and forward. This places my right elbow above Mark's left elbow.

Once I get my right elbow over the top of Mark's left elbow, it becomes very difficult for him to block the strike. Continuing to rotate my shoulder circularly, I drive my weight forward and drop my elbow straight down into Mark's face.

OVER-THE-TOP-ELBOW (VARIATION)

When executing an over-the-top elbow, it is imperative that you fold your arm over your opponent's arm to prevent him from blocking the strike. If your opponent's senses are keen, he will defensively lift his arm before you can accomplish this. To hinder his defense, a good option is to latch on to his wrist with your opposite hand and pin it to his chest. With his blocking arm out of the picture, you have a clear path to your target.

I'm in Mark's full guard. He's controlling my wrists with his hands, trying to hinder me from punching.	With punching difficult due to Mark's wrist control, I reach my left hand across his body and latch onto his left wrist to set up an over the top elbow.	Pinning Mark's left wrist to his chest with my left hand, I throw my right elbow over his left arm.	Now that my right elbow is above Mark's left arm, I let go of his wrist. Continuing to rotate my shoulder circularly, I drive my weight forward and drop my elbow straight down into Mark's face.

UPPERCUT FROM GUARD

The uppercut is a difficult punch for your opponent to block because it sails up between his arms. This is true when you throw it from the standing position, as well as when you throw it from the top guard position. A lot of opponents lying on their back will regularly lift up their head to see what's going on. The moment they do this, I like to drive in a quick uppercut. You don't need to look up at your opponent before throwing the punch. You know that his head is connected to his shoulders, so just fire it straight up the middle. Just as with all techniques you utilize on the ground, you have to be on the lookout for submissions. In this case, particularly the arm bar.

I'm in Beach's full guard. He's controlling my head with his left hand to prevent me from posturing up and unloading with punches. Notice how I am pinning his right arm to the mat with my left hand.	Still controlling Beach's right arm with my left hand, I slide my right arm to the inside of his left arm.	Once I slide my right arm to the inside of Beach's left arm, I keep my arm snug against his chest and punch my fist straight up the middle, landing flush to his chin.

HAMMER FIST TO ELBOW COUNTER

When postured up in your opponent's guard, a good option is to rain down a plethora of strikes and work to pass. In reaction to this, your opponent might wrap a hand around the back of your head and attempt to pull you back down into his guard. As he does this, his face becomes vulnerable, and you can make use of that vulnerability by smashing a hammer fist into his nose and jaw. If your opponent is stubborn and refuses to release his grip on your head, a good tactic is to grab his wrist, remove his hand from your neck, and then throw an over-the-top elbow.

I'm in Reagan's full guard. To prevent me from posturing up and throwing straight punches at his face, he has assumed head and wrist control.

Because Reagan is controlling my head with his left arm, his face is unprotected. To capitalize on that vulnerability, I cock my right hand back.

I chop my fist and wrist down into Reagan's face.

Reagan refuses to release his hold on my head. Before he has a chance to break my posture back down, I latch onto his left wrist with my right hand.

I pull Reagan's hand away from my head and posture up. It is important to notice that I do not let go of his wrist.

Holding Reagan's left wrist with my right hand, I rotate my right shoulder to get my right elbow above his left arm. Once I achieve this, I drop my elbow toward his face.

Driving my weight forward and continuing to rotate my shoulder, I smash my elbow into Reagan's face.

I quickly return to my defensive posture.

ELBOW TO THIGH TO STRAIGHT RIGHT

To do damage to your opponent from the top guard position, you often have to get creative. In this sequence, I drop my elbow down to my opponent's thigh and then immediately follow up with a right hand to his face. By throwing my first strike low, I force my opponent to think about the bottom half of his body, which takes a portion of his focus away from his top half. Although the low/high striking concept works a little differently on the ground than it does in the standing position, it's still an excellent tactic to get inside your opponent's head and create openings.

I'm postured up in Mark's full guard.

I raise my right arm in preparation to throw a downward elbow to Mark's thigh.

Pulling my right arm straight down, I drive the tip of my right elbow into the top of Mark's left thigh.

Immediately after digging my elbow into Mark's thigh, I snap my right fist straight into his jaw.

FAKE OPEN GUARD TO OVERHAND

If you're in the top guard position and don't make an effort to pass, your opponent can focus more intently on defending your strikes and setting up a submission. You must always switch things up, and this technique is one of my favorite ways to accomplish that. By using a hand to pry your opponent's legs apart, you force him to focus on the lower half of his body. While he is concentrating on defending against a pass, you quickly come over the top with an overhand to his face.

I'm in Mark's full guard.

Twisting my body in a clockwise direction, I place my right hand on Mark's left leg and press down. My intentions aren't to open his guard, but rather to get him to focus on his legs rather than protecting his face.

The ploy works and Mark leaves his face wide open. I capitalize by coming over the top with a strong overhand right.

FAKE OVERHAND TO ELBOW

In this technique you throw your right arm high as if you are going to deliver an overhand to your opponent's face. The overhand is a powerful punch that is easy to see coming, and you can almost guarantee that your opponent will cover his head with his arms the moment your arm goes up. This allows you to abandon the overhand and drive an elbow straight down into his solar-plexus.

I'm in Beach's guard, preparing to fake an overhand right to set myself up for an elbow strike.

I arch my right arm over the top to sell the overhand.

As Beach lifts his left arm to block the overhand, I rotate my right arm in and prepare to drop a downward elbow to his sternum.

Dropping my weight and utilizing the momentum generated by the fake overhand, I drive the tip of my right elbow into Beach's solar-plexus.

OPEN GUARD TO OVERHAND

When you're postured up in an opponent's open guard, he will often place a leg in front of your body to hinder you from throwing strikes. In this technique, I'm grabbing a hold of my opponent's leg and moving it to the side. This not only clears a path to his face, but it also chambers my hand for the overhand. However, the idea is to catch your opponent with his hands down, and the best way to accomplish this is to avoid telegraphing the punch. When in open guard you have a lot of options other than striking. You could work to pass your opponent's guard or even stand up. If your opponent thinks you are utilizing one of those other options, it steals his focus away from protecting his face, allowing you to land a clean punch.

I'm in Reagan's open guard. He has posted his left foot on my right hip and brought his left knee in front of my body to hinder me from throwing punches at his head.

I drop my right hand down to Reagan's left ankle, and I place my left hand on top of his left knee.

I latch onto Reagan's left ankle with my right hand and remove his foot from my hip. Then I pull on his ankle with my right hand and push on his knee with my left hand. Notice how I am not telegraphing the punch.

Still pushing on Reagan's knee with my left hand, I let go of his ankle and throw an overhand right.

Because I managed to steer Reagan's focus away from protecting his face, I catch him off guard and land my right hand to his jaw.

To prevent Reagan from executing a submission, I quickly assume a defensive posture.

DEFENDING AGAINST THE GUILLOTINE FROM GUARD

There are a variety of ways that you can end up in a guillotine choke while trapped between your opponent's legs. Your opponent could wrap up your neck and pull guard as you shoot in. Your opponent could secure the guillotine from the clinch and then jump to the guard position. Your opponent could sit up from guard and try to synch it in. The bottom line is that there are a number of ways to land in this potentially compromising position, so you must understand the basic principles of how to defend.

A common mistake many fighters make is they try to back out of a guillotine choke, but most of the time this only locks the choke in tighter. Instead, you want to push your weight forward. If you train jiu-jitsu, you already know this, but it seems that way too many fighters forget this simple concept. Wrapping your arm around your opponent's head and driving your shoulder into his face takes away the majority of his leverage. If your opponent is inexperienced locking in the guillotine, he might attempt to hold on to it. Just be patient and wait it out because your opponent will accomplish little more than sending a rush of blood to his arms and gassing his body out.

Mark managed to catch me in a guillotine choke. I defend by wrapping my left arm all the way around his head, and then driving my left shoulder into his face by pushing off my right leg. It is important to note that I am driving my weight into the choke rather than trying to pull away from it.

I climb up to both feet and drive all of my weight through my left shoulder. Now that I have created the space and breathing room needed to work my way out of the choke, I begin the hand-war by grabbing Mark's left hand with my right hand.

I pry Mark's left hand away from my neck with my right hand.

Pulling my head out from underneath Mark's left arm, I sit back and regain my posture. It's now time to make Mark pay for trying to choke me.

STRIKING PAST THE GUARD

I often see fighters who just sit in their opponent's guard without attempting to strike or pass. This will accomplish little more than getting the fight stood up, so you must stay active. It doesn't matter if your opponent is excellent at holding on and stalling when you're in his guard, you've got to keep busy. Sometimes this requires that you open his guard. You can accomplish this by utilizing one of the striking combinations I showed on the previous pages or work up to your feet as I do in this technique. It's much harder for your opponent to keep his legs locked when you're standing, and when you add downward punches to his face into the picture, he will almost always open his guard to get his defense going. If he doesn't open his legs while under fire, it usually doesn't take much to pry his legs apart. Once you open your opponent's guard, it puts you in a perfect position to pass, land some heavy strikes, or both.

I'm postured up in Reagan's full guard.

As I reach forward and grab Reagan's neck with my left hand, I lift my left knee and post my foot on the mat. If I had grabbed Reagan's neck with my right hand, I would have lifted my right knee and posted on my right foot. Executing both actions on the same side prevents your opponent from locking in an arm bar on your extended arm. Although it might still look like you're vulnerable, when you follow this rule your opponent won't be able to turn his hips to create the angle he needs for the submission.

Driving my left hand into Reagan's neck, I come up onto both feet.

Reagan keeps his guard closed. In an effort to get him to open his guard, I cock my right hand back and prepare to throw a straight right hand at his face.

I smash my right hand into Reagan's face.

As I cock my right hand back to land another blow, Reagan unhooks his legs to get his defense going.

Now that I've opened Reagan's guard, I work to control his legs. I start by grabbing his left ankle with my right hand.

I grab a hold of Reagan's right ankle with my left hand. For the best control, you want to grab slightly above your opponent's heels.

Turning my hips in a clockwise direction, I toss Reagan's legs to my right side. Notice how this sets me up for a big right hand.

Rotating my hips in a counterclockwise direction, I drop my weight and throw an overhand right at Reagan's face.

Dropping my body down with the overhand, I land on my knees and begin securing the side control position.

OPEN GUARD STACK PASS SEQUENCE

When in your opponent's guard you can use strikes to set up a pass, as well as use a pass to set up strikes. In this sequence, you're going to do both. Although your primary goal will be to escape your opponent's guard and transition to a more dominant position, he is bound to throw road blocks in your path. You can attempt to surmount the blockades using pure jiu-jitsu, but adding striking into the mix makes the task a whole lot easier to manage. The specific strikes shown below are just to get your mind going in the striking direction while executing your pass. There are a plethora of different strikes you can utilize, and deciding which ones to employ will largely depend upon how your opponent reacts to your pass.

I'm postured up in Beach's guard, working to open his legs to set up a pass.

Beach keeps his legs locked tight, refusing to open his guard. Instead of trying to pry his legs apart using my arms, I open his guard by throwing a straight right hand to his face.

The impact of the punch forces Beach's legs apart. The instant they open, I sit back onto my right foot and pop my left knee up. This not only prevents Beach from hooking his feet back together and closing his guard, but it also gives me the separation I need to get my arms underneath his legs.

The moment I sit back onto my right foot, I scoop both of my arms underneath Beach's legs. It is very important that steps 4 through 8 are done in one fluid motion because your opponent has the ability to punch you in the face.

Scooping Beach's legs up onto my shoulders, I squeeze my arms tightly around his thighs and grip my hands together. Then I pull his hips up onto my knees to limit his mobility.

Posting on my left foot and driving my weight forward, I dig my right forearm into Beach's neck. This not only makes him very uncomfortable, but it also gives me the positioning I need to pass.

STRIKING PAST THE GUARD

Posturing up, I drive my left knee into Beach's lower back to hold his hips in place and keep him propped up on his shoulders. I then cock my right hand back to land a punch to his face.

Before making my transition to side control, I throw my right hand between Beach's legs and crash my fist into his jaw.

Rotating my hips in a counterclockwise direction, I retract my right arm from between Beach's legs, hook my right arm around the outside of his left leg, and drive my forearm back down into his face.

Dropping my weight and flattening Beach out on his back, I sprawl my legs back to establish side control. It is important to notice that my left arm is still hooked underneath his hips, and that I've slid my right elbow down to the right side of his face.

HALF STACK PASS SEQUENCE

Sometimes it's difficult to scoop both arms underneath your opponent's legs when attempting the stack pass. If you manage to get one arm in and not the other, this technique and the technique that follows are two passing options you can utilize. Deciding which option to use will depend upon your opponent. Usually you will be able to feel which side he is weaker on based upon his resistance. In this sequence, my opponent is applying pressure with his downed leg, making passing to my left difficult. As a result, I pass to my right. Whichever technique you employ, it is important that you do so without lagging. Both of your hands will be tied up, which means your opponent can rabbit punch you in the face or land elbow strikes.

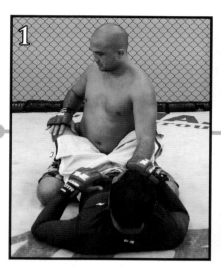

I'm postured up in Beach's guard, working to open his legs to set up a pass.

Beach keeps his legs locked tight, refusing to open his guard. Instead of trying to force his legs open with my hands, I throw an over-the-top elbow to his face.

The impact of the elbow strike forces Beach's legs apart. The instant they open, I sit back onto my right foot and pop my left knee up. Not only does this prevent Beach from hooking his feet back together and closing his guard, but it also gives me the separation I need to get my arms underneath his legs.

Beach keeps his right leg tight, making it difficult to hook my left arm underneath it. As a result, I decide to utilize the half stack pass and circle to my right. I begin by controlling his right leg with my left arm, and then scooping my right arm underneath his left leg.

Forcing Beach's right leg to the mat with my left hand, I place my left knee on top of his leg to keep it pinned. As I do this, I flare my right arm out to get Beach's left leg up onto my shoulder.

Keeping Beach's right leg pinned to the mat with my left knee, I reach my right hand across his body to his right shoulder. I also begin to press my weight forward, which will allow me to circle in a counterclockwise direction and pass his guard.

Posting on my left foot, I drive my weight forward and press my right arm into Beach's neck. As I do this, I circle my body in a counterclockwise direction in an attempt to pass his guard. To prevent me from circling, Beach places his left hand on my right hip.

Instead of peeling Beach's hand off my hip, I lift my right arm to drop a hammer fist to his face.

I drop my right arm and crash the sharp part of my wrist into Beach's face.

Landing the hammer fist forces Beach to focus less on stopping the pass and more on guarding himself from punches. The resistance he's applying to my hip lessens, and I quickly reposition my right arm across his neck and drive off my left leg to press my weight forward.

Still rotating in a counterclockwise direction, I drive my weight into Beach's face and drop my right hip toward the mat.

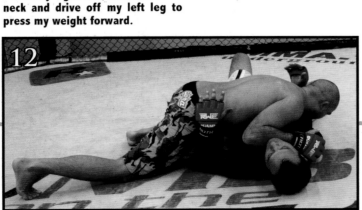

Continuing to circle in a counterclockwise direction, Beach's left leg passes underneath me. To assume side control, I move my left arm over to Beach's right side and drive my weight down on top of him.

THE GROUND GAME

HALF STACK PASS OVER THE LEG (OPTION 2)

As I mentioned in the previous move, the direction you choose to go with the half stack pass will depend upon the resistance you receive from your opponent. In the sequence below, my opponent is providing resistance on my under-hook side, which makes passing to my right difficult. As a result, I pass to my left over his downed leg. You shouldn't try to force either option, rather feel it out and constantly switch back and forth between the two until one pans out.

1 I'm preventing Beach from putting me back in his closed guard by sitting back on my right foot and keeping my left knee up.

2 As I drive my weight forward, Beach tightens up his left leg. I feel the resistance on my right shoulder, which tells me I should pass over his right leg. To do this, I drop my left knee over Beach's right leg and press my right foot into his right ankle. This last action prevents him from capturing me in his half guard.

3 Continuing to drive my weight forward, I step my right leg out from between Beach's legs and circle my body in a clockwise direction.

4 Having passed Beach's guard, I drop my hips to the mat and secure side control.

STRIKING PAST THE GUARD

BUTTERFLY PASS

When in your opponent's butterfly guard, this is a simple yet effective way to pass. All you are doing is softening your opponent up with strikes, shooting one leg back to clear his hooks from your hips, pushing his legs to the side, and then coming back into him to claim the side control position.

1 I'm in Troy's butterfly guard, and he has double under-hooks.

2 I throw a chopping punch into the back of Troy's head to get him thinking about defending punches instead of blocking my pass.

3 I pull my right hand back to land another blow.

4 This time I throw a chopping punch to Troy's ribs.

5 Having stolen Troy's focus away from defending my pass, I maintain a sturdy base and step my left leg back. Notice how this takes away the hooks he had on my hips. Immediately I use my hands to push Troy's knees to my left so I can clear my body around his legs and establish side control.

6 Having pushed Troy's legs to my left, I bring my left knee forward and press it into the back of his legs. This makes it very difficult for him to pull me back into his butterfly guard.

7 Bringing my right leg forward and posting my foot on the mat, I press my chest into Troy to flatten him out on his side.

8 Sitting up, I place my left hand on the side of Troy's head to keep him pinned to the mat. I can now begin dropping downward punches with my right hand.

MIKE PYLE SPECIAL

Earlier in the book I demonstrated how you can mess with your opponent's legs to steal his focus away from defending his face. Here you are going to mess with your opponent's face to steal his focus from his legs. Sitting up, you want to throw a punch at your opponent's head to get his attention. The moment you lift your hand to throw a second punch, your opponent will most likely cover his face and briefly forget about his legs. This often creates an opportunity to quickly pass your opponent's guard.

I'm in Paco's butterfly guard.

I posture up and cock my right hand back.

I throw a straight right hand to Paco's face.

Cocking my right hand back again, I act as though I'm going to come down with another punch. In order to get the pass, you must really sell the punch.

Instead of throwing the punch, I work for the pass by dropping my weight, pushing on Paco's right leg with my left hand, and posting my right hand on the mat by his left hip.

Continuing to push on Paco's right leg with my left hand, I swing my right leg in a clockwise direction to pass his guard. When stepping your leg out, it is important that you distribute your weight over your opponent to make a clean transition into side control.

I plant my right foot behind my left leg. Notice how I have dropped my weight into Paco's midsection to keep his body pinned to the mat.

I slide my left leg underneath my right and then flatten my hips on the mat, securing the side control position.

GUARD BOTTOM

I've seen many excellent jiu-jitsu practitioners forget about submissions and sweeps when they find themselves in the bottom guard position in MMA competition. Instead of working their jiu-jitsu, they throw an assortment of strikes in an attempt to knock their opponent out. It wouldn't be so bad if they used strikes to help set up submissions, but often times they don't. They simply get comfortable striking from their back. Unless you land a strike just right or get extremely lucky and manage to open a cut, you generally aren't going to end a fight with strikes while lying on your back. You can irritate your opponent, you can force movement with strikes, but usually the only way you can end a fight from the bottom guard position is with a submission. For this reason, you should think of the bottom guard in straight jiu-jitsu terms. You have to tailor your jiu-jitsu to deal with incoming strikes, but your goals on the bottom should be purely jiu-jitsu oriented. The three goals you want to work for are a submission, a sweep, and an escape back to your feet. It is important to focus on all three, not just submissions. If you're up against a good ground and pound fighter who is a master at slipping out of submissions, he is going to make you pay every time a submission attempt fails. If you don't use the movement your submission attempts generate to set up a sweep or an escape, you can quickly wind up a bloody mess.

Sit-Up Guard

When an opponent postures up in your guard, his ability to lock in a submission is greatly reduced, while his ability to land strikes greatly increases. He can throw an assortment of punches, as well as pin your head to the mat and land brutal elbow strikes. Not wanting to be on the receiving end of a beating, I will usually sit up with my opponent by posting on one arm, and then drive my opposite elbow into his neck, face, and chin. Because I close the distance between us, it greatly reduces his ability to land strikes. He can still get off some punches to my body, but they certainly aren't those devastating elbows to the face.

If your opponent should capitalize on his ability to throw body blows when you're playing the sit up guard, it shouldn't always be considered a negative. As long as your opponent is striking, he can't hold you, which means you have mobility. Since you are already up on one arm, you can sometimes make a quick escape back to your feet when your opponent strikes. The whole idea behind the sit-up guard is to take the least amount of punishment while still working toward bettering your positioning. As you will see in the upcoming section, there are many options at your disposal, and most of them work hand in glove with one another.

A Damn Good Guard

When an opponent postures up in your guard, the sit-up guard is a great option to utilize because it eliminates space and makes it very difficult for your opponent to land solid blows. However, not every opponent who wants to do damage with strikes from the top guard position will posture up. If your opponent likes throwing strikes while keeping his weight pressed down on top of you, it is critical that you open your guard and get your knees involved. You have to make your opponent hesitant to strike for fear of getting caught in a submission, and the best way to do that is to put yourself into a position where submissions become possible. The "damn good guard" is such a position, and it can save you from getting beaten into oblivion. By opening your guard and involving your legs, you open up a ton of submissions. If you fail to secure the "damn good guard" and your opponent postures up, you can immediately come up with him and play the sit-up guard.

Drills

Staying active in your guard is sometimes hard to manage. In order to get comfortable working your jiu-jitsu when your opponent is throwing downward strikes, it is important to constantly drill such a scenario in training. Have a training partner climb into your guard and work his ground and pound. All he can do is throw strikes, and all you can do is work for a sweep, a sub, or an escape back to your feet. If your opponent postures up, sit up with him. Once there, you can work your jiu-jitsu from the sit up guard or break him back down.

It is important to drill with as many different types of fighters as possible. Every competitor you face will behave differently when he is in your guard, and there are many different styles of ground and pound. There are guys like Mark Coleman, who will try and beat you up with his posture broken down, and there are guys like Caol Uno, who will try to posture up and ground and pound. There are fighters completely content staying in your closed guard and striking, and there are fighters who will use striking to pass your guard into a more dominant position. You have to train with all different kinds of fighters to learn what works best for you in any given situation.

Key Concepts for Guard Bottom

✓Always be working for three things: A sweep, a submission, or getting back to your feet.
✓Keep your opponent extremely close to you or far away.
✓If your opponent postures up, you can utilize the sit-up guard or break him back down and work from the clinch.
✓If nothing is working for you from closed guard, open your legs and make something happen from open guard.

SIT-UP GUARD

Any time you find yourself in the bottom guard position, you want to lock in a submission, sweep your opponent, or escape up to your feet. These are your three goals. When your opponent postures up in your guard, playing the sit-up guard not only allows you to work for these goals, but it can also save you from taking an unnecessary beating. In the photos below, I demonstrate how to establish the sit-up guard when your opponent postures up.

Troy is postured up in my closed guard.

Immediately I shoot my left arm up to the left side of Troy's head and come up onto my right elbow.

Driving the sharp side of my wrist into Troy's neck, I continue to sit up and post on my right hand. From this position I can not only avoid getting hit with damaging elbows to the face, but I can also escape up to my feet, transition to Troy's back, or set up submissions.

GETTING UP 101

A lot of people wonder how I get up from the bottom guard position when the fight goes to the ground. The answer is I utilize this technique. It's one of the first moves that you learn in jiu-jitsu, but a lot of jiu-jitsu practitioners don't practice it on a regular basis because they are content working off their backs, which often gets them into trouble in MMA. In order to become effective with this move, you must incorporate it into your training. Have a partner pin you down and unleash with ground and pound while you utilize this technique to get back to your feet. If you practice it again and again, eventually it will become second nature.

Troy is postured up in my closed guard.

Immediately I shoot my left arm up to the left side of Troy's head and come up onto my right elbow.

Driving the sharp side of my wrist into Troy's neck, I continue to sit up and post on my right hand.

Driving my left arm into Troy's neck, I unhook my feet and post my left foot on the mat. This allows me to elevate my hips, as well as turn them in a clockwise direction.

Driving my left hand into Troy's head to create space, I push off my left leg, further elevate my hips, and begin pulling my right leg out.

Still driving my left hand into Troy's face, I pull my right leg out and plant it on the mat behind me.

Posting on my right foot, I pull my left leg back to create more space between Troy and I. To prevent him from shooting in for the takedown, I continue to hold him at bay with my left hand.

Pushing Troy away, I back all the way out and assume my fighting stance.

BASIC HIP SWEEP

The basic hip sweep is an excellent technique because it flips your opponent over to his back and lands you in the mount. If your opponent should block the sweep by dropping his weight or posting his arm, it sets you up for a either a guillotine or kimura. Below I demonstrate the sweep, and on the coming pages I show the submissions based on your opponent's counters to the sweep.

I've achieved the sit up guard position by driving my left arm into Troy's neck, sitting up, and posting on my right hand. Right now my body is loaded like a spring, and in order to get the sweep, all I have to do is explosively turn by hips and scissor my legs.

Unhooking my feet, I post my left leg on the mat and elevate my hips. As I jam my left hip up into Troy's right armpit, I turn my body in a clockwise direction.

Continuing to turn my shoulders and hips in a clockwise direction, I wrap my left arm over Troy's left arm. In addition to helping me carry him over with the sweep, it also prevents him countering the technique by posting his left hand on the mat.

Because I was explosive with my movements, Troy gets swept over to his back.

As Troy comes down to his back, I land in the mount position.

KIMURA FROM SIT UP GUARD

If you step toward your opponent and throw a single punch, the chances are he will either block it or step out of the way. But when you unleash with a savage combination, your opponent will have a much harder time evading all of your strikes. The same concept applies on the ground. In this scenario, I attempt a basic hip sweep, my opponent counters by posting his arm, and I immediately use his defensive movement against him by abandoning the sweep and transitioning into a Kimura.

I've achieved the sit up guard position by sitting up, posting on my right hand, and driving the sharp part of my left wrist into Troy's neck.

Unhooking my feet, I post my left leg on the ground and elevate my hips. As I jam my left hip up into Troy's right armpit, I turn my body in a clockwise direction.

Troy posts his left hand on the mat, countering the sweep. I immediately hook my left arm over his left arm to apply the Kimura.

I drop down to my right elbow and latch onto Troy's left wrist with my right hand.

Reaching my left arm underneath Troy's left arm, I grab the top of my right wrist with my left hand. As I do this, I turn my hips in a counterclockwise direction and roll to my back. It is important to notice that as I come down onto my back, I scoot my hips to my right side. This gives me the angle that I need to really crank down on the Kimura.

Rolling over onto my left shoulder, I throw my right leg over Troy's back to keep his posture broken and rotate my body so it is perpendicular to his. To finish the Kimura, I pull my left arm into my body while driving my right arm in the direction of Troy's head. This puts a tremendous amount of pressure on his left shoulder.

POSTURE UP TO GUILLOTINE

A lot of times when you execute a basic hip sweep, your opponent will counter by dropping his weight down into you. If he exposes his neck in the process, which happens quite often, you have the option of going for a guillotine choke. Even if you don't get it, you force your opponent to defend, and this can often set you up for another technique. Remember, the more techniques you throw at your opponent, the better chance you have of getting one step ahead of him. When you go for the choke but can't lock it in, move on to something else instead of wasting your energy.

Posting on my right elbow, I drive my left arm into the left side of Mark's neck.

Continuing to drive my left arm into Mark's neck, I sit all the way up and post on my right hand.

Unhooking my feet, I post my left foot on the mat and elevate my hips. As I jam my left hip up into Troy's right armpit, I turn my body in a clockwise direction.

Mark counters the sweep by wrapping his arms around my hips and driving his weight forward.

Although continuing with the sweep would be difficult, Mark has dropped his head to drive his weight into me, giving me an opportunity to sink in a guillotine choke. I begin by wrapping my left arm around the back of his head and sneaking my left hand underneath his chin.

Rolling onto my back, I dig my right arm between our bodies and latch onto my left wrist with my right hand. It is very important to note that my right arm is in front of Mark's left arm. If you place your arm behind your opponent's arm, it becomes very difficult to lock in the choke.

To lock in the choke, I lock my feet together, squeeze my arms tight, and extend my legs to help dig my forearm into Mark's neck.

POSTURE UP TO OMAPLATA

When you execute the basic hip sweep and your opponent counters by wrapping his arms around your legs and driving you back down, you have the option of going for the omaplata. If your opponent is covered in Vaseline or both of you are soaked in sweat, the submission can sometimes be hard to lock in due to the slip factor, but you can often use the movement your submission attempt generated to claim the top position or escape back to your feet.

Posting on my right elbow, I drive my left arm into the left side of Troy's neck.

Continuing to drive my left arm into Troy's neck, I sit all the way up, unhook my feet, and post on my right hand.

I post my left foot on the ground and elevate my hips. As I jam my left hip up into Troy's right armpit, I turn my body in a clockwise direction.

Troy counters the sweep by wrapping his arms around my legs and driving his weight forward.

Although continuing with the sweep will be difficult, Troy has wrapped his arms around my legs, creating an opportunity for me to lock in the omaplata. As Troy tackles me forward, I swing my hips in a counterclockwise direction, roll to my back, and swing my right leg over his left arm.

I trap Troy's left arm against my right thigh using my right hand, and then I begin to pull my left leg out from underneath his body.

As I sit up, I post on my left hand, continue to scoot my hips out, and begin sliding my left leg underneath me. As I do this, I straighten my right leg to pin Troy's left shoulder to the mat.

Coiling my right leg in and my left leg back, I sit all the way up, wrap my right arm under Troy's right arm, wrap my left arm underneath his head, and grip my hands together. To finish the submission, I drive Troy's left shoulder down with my right leg and pull his forearm upward by elevating my hips.

POSTURE UP TO ARM BAR

When you play the sit-up guard, you hinder your opponent's offensive options. In order to get something going, your opponent will often attempt to drive your body back to the mat with his hands. If you time it right, you can use his force against him by trapping his arm, rolling to your back, throwing your leg over his head, and securing an arm bar. Even if you don't lock in the submission, your opponent will be forced to defend, and his movement will often create an opportunity for you to escape back to your feet or set up another submission.

Posting on my right elbow, I drive my left arm into the left side of Mark's neck.

Before I sit up and post on my right hand, Mark brings his arms to the inside of my body and begins to drive my body back to the mat.

Rather than resist Mark's downward pressure, I willingly fall to my back. As I do this, I hook my right hand around the inside of his left thigh. This hook will help me rotate my hips in a counterclockwise direction and get the angle I need to secure the arm bar.

Using my right hook on Mark's left leg, I pull my body in a counterclockwise direction. As I rotate, I start to maneuver my left leg around to the left side of Mark's head. It is important to notice how I am using my left arm to keep Mark's head at a distance, which helps me get my leg around.

I swing my left leg around to the left side of Mark's head.

I drop my left arm and pin Mark's right arm flat to my chest. To finish the arm bar, I apply downward pressure with both legs, squeeze my knees together, and extend my hips upward.

SIT-UP GUARD

SIT UP GUARD TO BACK

When you play the sit-up guard, your opponent's only real striking option is to punch or elbow you with his near arm. If he capitalizes on that option, a good tactic is to slip your head underneath the strike as it comes at you. As the downward momentum of your opponent's strike carries his body toward the mat, you hook the arm you have dug into his neck around his shoulder. This gives you the leverage to pull yourself out from underneath his body and climb onto his back. I'm not going to lie and say that it is an easy move to pull off, but it can certainly be accomplished.

Posting on my right elbow and driving my left arm into the side of Beach's face, I see him draw his left arm back to land an elbow strike to my face.

Beach drives his left arm forward to land an elbow strike to my face. As I dodge the blow by ducking my head, I hook my left hand behind his left shoulder. The instant his elbow sails by my head, I force him to overcommit to the strike by using my hook on his shoulder to pull down on his body.

Using my hook on Beach's shoulder to drive his face into the mat, I post my right foot on the mat and scoot my hips out to my right side.

Continuing to pull down on Beach's shoulder and scoot my hips out, I push off my right leg and reach my right arm over Beach's back.

I hook my right hand on the side of Beach's body and throw my right leg over his back. To help climb on top of him, I push off my left arm. It is important to notice that as I throw my right leg over his back, I hook my left leg around the inside of his left leg, securing my first hook.

To establish my second hook and secure the back position, I sneak my right foot to the inside of Beach's right hip. It is important to notice how I lace my right arm underneath Beach's right arm. This helps prevent him from bucking me off.

SIT UP GUARD TO BACK (OPTION 2)

As I mentioned, your opponent will be limited to striking with his near arm when you're in the sit-up guard. If he utilizes that option and you don't see the punch until it's already coming toward you, your best bet for taking his back is to use the previous technique. However, playing the sit-up guard often allows you to read your opponent's movements due to the body-to-body contact. If you feel your opponent loading his near arm up for a big punch or elbow, a good option is to shoot both your arm and head underneath his arm the moment he lifts it up to strike. This allows you to scoot your hips out from underneath him and create the angle you need to pull yourself up onto his back. I used this technique during my second fight with Matt Hughes in the UFC. Although it worked flawlessly, I ended up tearing my ribs apart as I spun around to his back. Despite this injury, it's still an excellent move.

1 I've achieved the sit up guard position by driving my left arm into Beach's neck, sitting up, and posting on my right hand.

2 Beach raises his left arm to drop an elbow to my face. The moment he does this, I slip my left arm underneath his arm and lean to my right side so I can create the necessary angle to make my transition.

3 As Beach drops his downward elbow, I guide it over my head using my left arm. Notice how this forces Beach down to the mat. Then I sit up and wrap my left arm over his back.

Posting on my left hand and right foot, I push off the mat and scoot my hips out from underneath Beach's body. I use my right hand to help pull my body up onto his back so I can establish my right hook.

Throwing my right leg over Beach's back, I sneak my right foot to the inside of his right hip and establish my second hook. It is important to notice how I lace my right arm underneath his arm. This gives me the control I need to mount an attack.

GETTING UP FROM GUARD

This is a great way to get back to your feet when an opponent attempts to posture up in your guard to deliver downward strikes. Since you already have one hand behind your opponent's head, you can use his posturing-up momentum to help pull yourself up onto your elbow. Once on your elbow, you want to come up onto your hand. And once you're up on your hand, you want to pull your leg out from underneath your opponent and work back to your feet. Although it's a rather simple technique, it works surprisingly well.

I've got Albert in my closed guard. I'm keeping his posture broken down by controlling his head with my left arm.

Albert attempts to posture up by lifting his head and pushing off my chest with both hands. Instead of burning energy trying to hold him down, I decide to use his upward momentum to get back to my feet.

Because I'm still gripping Albert's head with my left arm, his upward momentum helps pull me up to my right elbow.

Continuing to sit up, I come up onto my right hand and post my left foot on the mat. Pushing off my left foot, I elevate my hips off the mat and pull my right leg back.

Pulling my right leg behind me and posting my right foot on the mat, I stand up. Notice how I still have my left hand wrapped around Albert's head. In addition to helping me block punches, it also allows me to control distance.

As I stand all the way up, I push Albert away from me to complete my escape.

I assume my standard fighting stance.

STANDARD GUARD TACTICS

KICK OUT TO STANDING

A lot of opponents like to remain postured down in your guard and work ground and pound. Although it is hard for your opponent to do any real damage when striking from this position, he will still be winning the fight in the eyes of the judges. To make something happen, you might have to open your guard and kick your opponent away from you. By creating separation, you gain the opportunity to snap back to your feet. It's a great move for strikers because you don't have to be a jiu-jitsu black belt to pull it off. All you really need to understand is how to create space and properly get back to your feet.

1

I've got Troy in my closed guard. I'm controlling his head with my left arm to keep him from posturing up.

2

I maneuver my left hand to the left side of Troy's head.

3

Unhooking my feet, I drive Troy's head to my left side using my left hand. At the same time, I hook my right hand around the inside of his left leg.

4

Continuing to push on Troy's head with my left hand, I drive my right leg into his left side. As I do this, I use my right hook on his left leg to help pull my hips out from underneath his body, strip his base, and force him off balance.

5

Still driving my right leg into Troy to prevent him from turning back into my guard, I slide my left leg out from underneath him and wedge my foot into his left armpit.

6

I wedge my left foot deeper into Troy's armpit and use that base to begin shoving his body away.

7

Shoving Troy away from me with my left foot, I use that outward momentum to sit up and begin working back to my feet.

8

As I sit all the way up, I post on my right hand and left foot. This allows me to scoot my right leg underneath my body. To gauge distance and guard myself from punches, I keep my left arm extended.

9

Pushing off my left leg, I post my right foot behind me and stand up. I keep my left arm extended to guard against punches and gauge distance. From here I will transition into my standard fighting stance.

BLOCKING THE OVERHAND

When an opponent postures up in your guard, playing the sit-up guard is a good option because it hinders his ability to land strikes. However, sometimes your opponent may prevent you from sitting up by posting his hands on your stomach and keeping you pinned to the mat. Such a situation is not optimal because it sets your opponent up for a big overhand punch to your face. If your opponent cocks his arm back for that punch, a good defensive option is to keep your feet hooked together and explode your knees toward your chest as if you were doing a crunch. This shatters your opponent's base, which not only takes power away from his punch, but also causes him to fall down on top of you. To further block the punch, you want to shoot your arm up as you bring your knees in. Once you've blocked the punch and your opponent has fallen forward, you can use the arm you blocked with to secure an over-hook. From there, a good option is to transition into the "damn good guard" and start working your triangle and omaplata setups.

Albert is postured up in my full guard. He has posted his hands on my stomach to prevent me from sitting up into him.

Albert cocks his right arm back to deliver an overhand punch.

As Albert comes down with the punch, I raise my left hand to the inside of his arm. At the same time, I pull my legs into me to thrust Albert forward.

STANDARD GUARD TACTICS

I straighten my left arm. This not only blocks the punch, but it also creates an opportunity to trap Albert's right arm with an over-hook.

The momentum of Albert's punch drops his torso down on top of me. I immediately wrap my left arm around his right arm to secure an over-hook. Albert's posture is now broken, and I have an over-hook on my left side.

BLOCKING OVERHAND TO A DAMN GOOD GUARD

If your opponent is content staying in your guard and working ground and pound, utilizing your legs to block his punches is an excellent strategy. You should still be moving and working for a sweep, submission, or an escape back to your feet, but if you can't block the strikes coming your way, you won't get very far with your attacks. The best way to get your legs involved is to place one leg on your opponent's back to keep him postured down and place your opposite knee in front of his shoulder to eliminate his ability to throw hard strikes. Getting a knee in front of his shoulder can prove difficult when he is lying on top of you, but any-time he rears back for a big punch, you'll usually have the space needed to bring your knee toward your chest and wedge it in front of his shoulder. It's important that once you block your opponent's strike, you immediately start to make your transition into the "damn good guard" by securing an over-hook.

I've got Beach broken down in my closed guard. It's important to notice that I'm controlling his posture by keeping my left arm wrapped around his head. You want to maintain this control throughout the entire sequence to prevent your opponent from sitting up and generating power behind his punches.

Beach cocks his left hand back to land a big overhand to my face. The instant he does this, I open my guard and jam my right knee in front of his left shoulder. For insurance purposes, I also lift my right hand to catch the punch if it should sneak past my leg.

My right knee stops Beach's overhand punch before it reaches my face. From here, I will most likely work for an over-hook on Beach's right arm and establish The Damn Good Guard position (p. 208).

ELBOWS FROM CLOSED GUARD

Lying on your back isn't the optimal position from which to strike, but you've still got some options. You can land open palm strikes to your opponent's ears in hopes of damaging his eardrums, and you can strike his kidneys with your heels. But perhaps your best striking option is to land an elbow to your opponent's head. The optimal time to use this technique is when your opponent is stalling on top of you or while he's trying to stabilize his position after taking you down. Placing both hands on his head, you want to force his head to one side with your arms. His reaction will most likely be to drive his head back into you. The moment he does this, you release his head. As his head snaps back toward you, unleash the elbow strike. You probably won't get the knockout, but it's quite possible to open a cut. At the very least, you will create movement.

Troy has his head down in my closed guard.

I maneuver both hands to Troy's face and push his head away from me to create space.

As I let go of Troy's head, his head snaps back into me and I throw my right elbow into his temple.

I follow through with the elbow to cause the most damage.

I immediately pull my right arm out from underneath Troy.

KNEE-PUNCH ARM BAR

When your opponent stalls in the top guard position with his elbows pinched tightly to your hips, it can be difficult to create movement to get something going. If you can't pull your opponent's arm to the center of your chest to set up an arm bar (an arm bar is only possible when your opponent's elbow is to the inside of your hips), the knee-punch arm bar is an excellent alternative. It bears this name because you use your knee to force your opponent's elbow toward the center of your chest, which allows you to set up the arm bar. If your opponent feels you going for the arm bar and pulls his arm out, then you can immediately transition into the triangle, which is the next technique in this section. With this technique and the one that follows, it is very important to hook your arm under your opponent's leg because it allows you to turn your body and assume the necessary angle to finish the submissions.

Beach is in my full guard, keeping his arms locked tight to my sides.

I place both hands on the left side of Beach's face and push his head to my left.

Here I do several things at once. I continue to drive Beach's head to my left side using my left hand; I hook my right arm around the inside of Beach's left leg; I open my guard and shrimp my hips in a counterclockwise direction; and I maneuver my right leg up toward Beach's left shoulder.

Applying downward pressure on Beach's back with my right leg to prevent him from posturing up, I begin to swing my left leg around his head. As my left leg travels in a counterclockwise direction, it forces Beach's right elbow toward the center of my chest, which will allow me to work for the arm bar. It is important to notice that I'm maintaining outward pressure on Beach's head with my left hand to throw off his base and create the angle I need to swing my leg around his head.

As my left leg swings around to the front of Beach's head, his right arm is forced toward the center of my chest. It is important to notice that I'm still pushing on his head with my left hand and applying downward pressure on his back with my right leg.

I swing my left leg around to the front of Beach's head, which traps his right arm between my legs.

I reach my left arm across my body and trap Beach's right hand in the crook of my elbow. To finish the arm bar, I apply downward pressure with both legs, elevate my hips, and pull Beach's right arm down into my chest.

PULL OUT OF ARM BAR TO TRIANGLE

When you utilize the knee-punch arm bar on an opponent who is stalling in the top guard position, there is a good chance that he will recognize your intentions the moment you force his arm toward the center of your chest. If your opponent defends against the submission by ripping his arm free, he will need to plant his hand on the mat to regain his base. This allows you to transition straight into the triangle choke. It's a perfect example of how analyzing your opponent's possible reactions to an attack can allow you to set up yet another attack. The more time you spend with this analyzation, the more lethal your combinations will become.

Beach is in my closed guard, keeping his arms locked tight to my sides.

I place both hands on the left side of Beach's face and push his head to my left.

Here I do several things at once. I continue to drive Beach's head to my left side using my left hand; I hook my right arm around the inside of Beach's left leg; I open my guard and shrimp my hips in a counterclockwise direction; and I maneuver my right leg up toward Beach's left shoulder.

Applying downward pressure on Beach's back with my right leg to prevent him from posturing up, I begin to swing my left leg around his head. As my left leg travels in a counterclockwise direction, it forces Beach's right elbow toward the center of my chest, which will allow me to work for the arm bar. It is important to notice that I'm maintaining outward pressure on Beach's head with my left hand to throw off his base and give me the angle I need to swing my leg around his head.

As I continue to maneuver my left leg around to the front of Beach's head to secure the arm bar, he counters by ripping his arm out from between my legs. Because I'm pushing his head to my left side, Beach is forced to post his right hand on the mat as soon as he pulls his arm free. This allows me to immediately transition to the triangle.

As Beach plants his right hand on the mat to secure his base, I wrap my left leg around the right side of his head. Then I slide my left leg underneath my right knee. To trap Beach's left arm across his neck, I fold my body in tight. This last step is very important for the triangle choke to work. If Beach had managed to get his left arm to the right side of my body, I would have grabbed his wrist with my left hand and pulled his arm underneath his neck.

To finish the triangle, I squeeze my knees together and pull down on Beach's head with both hands.

ARM TRAP TRIANGLE

The arm trap is a control position that I've seen both Eddie Bravo and Dean Lister utilize. It's an excellent position because in addition to disrupting your opponent's base, you also lock up one of his arms. Your opponent still has his other arm to strike with, but because you're pushing his head away from your body, it makes it difficult for him to generate any significant power behind his blows. In the photos below, I secure the arm trap and then quickly lock in a triangle as my opponent tries to punch with his free hand.

Mark is in my full guard. He has made the mistake of placing his hands on the mat, and I'm going to capitalize on that mistake by trapping his left hand to the canvas. I start by maneuvering my left arm to the left side of his head.

Bringing my right leg up toward Mark's left shoulder, I sit up and reach out with my right arm.

I reach my right arm around Mark's left arm and the back of my knee, and then I clasp my hands together over his left shoulder. This traps Mark's left arm, and his only real striking option is to punch me with his free hand. However, it is important to mention that I'm really squeezing my left leg into Mark's right side. If you do not manage a tight squeeze, your opponent can use his free hand to push your leg to the ground and pass your guard.

The instant Mark cocks his right hand back to fire a punch at my face, I capitalize on the newly created space by bringing my left leg underneath his right arm.

I throw my left leg over Mark's right shoulder.

I wrap my left leg around the back of Mark's head.

Unclasping my hands, I use my left leg to keep Mark's posture broken, and I use my right hand to pull my left foot behind my right knee.

I bring my left arm to the right side of Mark's head.

Wrapping my left arm around the back of my left knee, I grip my hands together over the top of my left leg so that my right palm is facing down. To finish the choke, I squeeze my legs tight and pull Mark's head down with my arms.

DAMN GOOD TRIANGLE

This technique is exactly what the title implies—a damn good triangle. Once you get your knee in front of your opponent's shoulder and secure an over-hook on the opposite side, there is very little your opponent can do in the way of offense. This allows you to immediately secure the triangle or land some strikes. The bottom line is that you don't end up in this superior position by playing closed guard. It's your job to make things happen, and that can only come about through movement.

Beach is in my full guard. Although his arms are locked tight to my side, he has made the mistake of placing his hands on the mat.

Immediately I take advantage of Beach's hands being on the mat by wrapping my left arm around his right arm, which gives me over-hook control on my left side.

Opening my guard, I bring my left leg up Beach's back and apply downward pressure to prevent him from posturing up. As I do this, I push his left arm down toward my legs with my right hand and work my right knee in front of his left shoulder.

Having established the Damn Good Guard position by bringing my right knee in front of Beach's left shoulder, I place my right hand on his head and push him away from me.

As Beach forces his head back into me, I quickly let go of his head and throw an elbow. Because he is driving his head toward me, the impact is greater.

Immediately after I land the elbow, I draw my right fist back.

With Beach unable to protect his head, I throw a chopping punch into his face.

Instead of pulling my right fist back to land another blow, I place my hand on Beach's face and force his head back and to my right. This creates enough space to slide my right leg out from underneath his left arm.

A DAMN GOOD GUARD

I wrap my right leg around the back of Beach's neck and then apply downward pressure to prevent him from posturing up and escaping the submission.

Maintaining downward pressure with my right leg, I maneuver my left leg around my right foot.

As I bring my left leg down over my right foot, I pull Beach's right arm across my body using my right hand.

To finish the triangle, I squeeze my knees together and pull down on Beach's head with both hands.

DAMN GOOD OMAPLATA

In this sequence I show how to lock in the omaplata from the "damn good guard" position. I prefer the triangle because it's easier to apply and has a higher success rate, but that doesn't mean that the omaplata isn't a damn good move. Just as with the "damn good triangle," it is imperative that you keep your over-hook tight and prevent your opponent from posturing up by maintaining downward pressure on his back with your leg.

I've got Butch trapped in the Damn Good Guard. To secure the position, I keep my left over-hook wrapped tight around his right arm and maintain downward pressure with my left leg to keep him from posturing up. I also grab his left wrist with my right hand for control purposes.

Releasing Butch's left hand, I cock my right fist back.

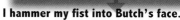
I hammer my fist into Butch's face.

A DAMN GOOD GUARD

Instead of cocking my fist back to land another strike, I plant my right hand on the right side of Butch's face and shove his head away from my body. This creates enough space between us for me to begin moving my left leg in front of his face.

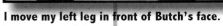

I move my left leg in front of Butch's face.

As I pull my right leg out from underneath Butch's body, I scoot my hips in a clockwise direction. To prevent him from freeing his right arm as I make my transition, I control his right wrist with my left hand.

Continuing to scoot my hips in a clockwise direction, I sit up and wrap my left arm over Butch's back. To pin his right shoulder to the mat, I straighten my left leg. The idea is to place as much weight as possible on your opponent's shoulder so he can't posture up and work for an escape.

Posting on my right foot, I coil my left leg in towards me and press my weight forward.

To finish the submission, I come down onto my right knee and lean forward. This puts a tremendous amount of pressure on Butch's right shoulder.

HOOKING THE ARM FROM OMAPLATA

There are a lot of things that can happen when you sit out to secure the omaplata submission. The ideal situation is to secure the shoulder lock right off the bat and get the finish, but it's not always that easy. If your opponent rolls as you sit up, you'll probably want to follow him over and secure side control. If your opponent postures up and turns into you, then you can immediately transition into the triangle or hook your foot underneath his far arm and break him back down, which is the technique I demonstrate below.

I've managed to get my hips out from underneath Albert and secure the omaplata control position.

Albert begins to posture up in an attempt to escape the omaplata submission.

As Albert postures up, I roll onto my back and hook my left foot underneath his right armpit.

To break Albert back down to the mat, I come up onto my left elbow and begin to straighten my left leg.

Straightening out my left leg, I break Albert's posture back down to the mat and cock my right hand back.

As I sit all the way up and post on my left hand, I drive my right fist into the back of Albert's head. From here I will most likely get my left leg out from underneath him and work to finish the omaplata.

THE SPIN AROUND

If you're in the bottom guard position and your opponent is dragging you toward the fence, bells and whistles should be sounding in your head, warning you of danger. Continuing to play closed guard won't save you. It's true that playing closed guard prevents your opponent from being able to pass your guard and achieve a more dominant position, but he still has the option of dropping down some deathblows. And those deathblows only get more lethal if he should get your head mashed up against the chain link. So if you're getting dragged toward the fence, you've got to open your guard and make something happen. Your best option is to get back to your feet, but when such an option isn't available, the Spin Around is a good technique to have as a backup.

Troy is in my guard attempting to drive my head against the cage.

Driving off his left foot, Troy pushes me closer to the cage.

As Troy comes down on his left knee, I hook my right hand around the inside of his left leg. This will help me spin my hips in a counterclockwise direction and avoid having my head pinned up against the cage.

As Troy brings his right leg forward and posts on his foot, I use my hook on his left leg to spin my hips in a counterclockwise direction almost as if I am going for an arm bar. To prevent him from driving me up against the cage, I post my left hand and leg on the fence. Although grabbing the fence is illegal in most MMA competitions, you can usually get away with it so long as you don't hold on for longer than a second.

Using my right hook on Troy's left leg, I continue to rotate in a counterclockwise direction so that my head is facing away from the cage. At the same time, I drive my right leg into his side to keep him between my legs.

Driving my right leg into Troy's side, he is forced to drop his weight and I close my guard by hooking my feet together.

GETTING UP AGAINST THE CAGE

Lying on your back with your head rammed against the cage is not a good position to be in. Many fighters have lost battles while stuck in this compromising position. If your opponent is a decent striker who understands how to do some damage from the top guard position, you need to get out of there even if it could result in taking some damage. Personally, I like to utilize this technique. Posting on one hand and foot, you snap up so that you're in a squat position with your back pressed up against the cage. Once you reach this position, your opponent basically has two options—he can grab a-hold of your legs and haul you back down or he can open up with strikes. Although the latter is never fun to endure, it certainly has its upside. Your opponent can't strike and hold on to your legs at the same time, so as long as you don't get knocked out, you will get back to you feet and escape a terrible position. You might take some abuse to get out of there, but at least you have a moving chance.

I'm pinned up against the cage with Troy in my full guard.

As Troy cocks his right hand back to land an overhand to my face, I maneuver my left hand to the left side of his head.

Driving my left arm into Troy, I unhook my feet, sit up to my right side, and come up onto my right elbow. Because of my movement, Troy no longer has the angle he needs to land the overhand.

Maintaining outward pressure with my left arm, I post on my right hand and left foot, slide my body out from underneath Troy, and elevate my hips off the mat.

Continuing to inch my hips back, I push off my left leg. This creates the elevation I need to draw my right leg in and place my right knee on the mat.

Still driving my left arm into Troy, I push off my left leg and begin working up to my feet.

I come up onto both feet.

Immediately I pummel my right arm under Troy's left arm to secure an under-hook.

I slide my left arm underneath Troy's right arm to secure my second under-hook. Although I just escaped a very bad position, I'm still not in a great spot because I'm pinned up against the cage. From here I will continue to work to improve my positioning with a reversal (p. 127).

PINNED AGAINST THE CAGE (HOOKING THE LEG)

When you're pinned up against the cage and attempt to escape to your feet using the previous technique, your opponent will often drive his weight into you in an attempt to haul you back to the mat. In such a situation, this basic wrestling technique can come to your rescue.

I'm pinned up against the cage with Troy in my full guard.

I maneuver my left hand to the left side of Troy's head.

Driving my left arm into Troy's head, I open my guard and post my left foot on the mat.

Maintaining outward pressure with my left arm, I post on my right hand and push off. This allows me to scoot my hips out from underneath Troy's body.

Pushing off my left foot and right hand, I create the separation I need to pull my right leg in.

I climb onto my right knee. Unable to work up to my feet because Troy is driving his weight into me, I hook my left arm around the inside of his left leg to set up the sweep.

Pushing off my left foot and using my hook on Troy's left leg, I scoot my hips out to my right side.

I continue to scoot around Troy in a counterclockwise direction using my hook on his left leg and by pushing off my left foot. Once you scoot all the way out and your body is perpendicular to your opponent's body, you can drive forward and sweep him over.

Sitting up, I swing my right leg back and reach my right arm over Troy's back.

I drive forward off my right foot and tackle Troy over.

Continuing to press forward, I push Troy over to his back.

GETTING UP FROM BUTTERFLY GUARD

When you have an opponent in your butterfly guard, you've got to sit up in order to get offensive. If your opponent manages to pin you flat on your back, you need to get your hooks underneath his hips, drive him away from you to relieve some of his weight from your body, and then sit up. Once achieved, your best option for advancing to a more dominant position is to execute a sweep. There are literally dozens of different sweeps that you can utilize from butterfly guard, but sweeps don't always work. It's beneficial to be able to escape back to your feet from whatever position you may find yourself in, and this technique is an excellent way to accomplish that from butterfly guard. I particularly like this escape for MMA because you keep one arm hooked around your opponent's body for the duration of the move, which greatly hinders your opponent's ability to sock you in the face as you pop back up to your feet.

I'm sitting up in the butterfly guard. I've established a left under-hook on Albert, and I'm controlling his left arm by grabbing his triceps with my right hand.

I place my right foot on Albert's left knee.

I drive my right foot into Albert's left knee, forcing his leg back and collapsing his base.

Posting on my right hand and left foot, I pull my right leg out from underneath Albert's body and elevate my hips off the ground. It is important that you make this transition before your opponent has time to reestablish his base.

Pulling my right leg back and posting on my foot, I come up to me feet. It is important to notice that I still have my left under-hook. As long as I have that under-hook, it will be very difficult for Albert to shoot in for my legs as I make the transition.

Standing all the way up, I prepare to push Albert away from me.

Pushing Albert away with my hands, I disengage and assume my fighting stance.

BUTTERFLY SWEEP (OPTION 1)

This is the first sweep that I'll utilize from the butterfly guard. All I'm doing in the photos below is sitting up, gripping my opponent's left triceps to prevent him from posting his arm, falling over to my side, and then sweeping him over to his back using my left under-hook and left butterfly hook. If you execute this sweep and your opponent counters by posting his leg on the mat, you can use his compromised positioning to sweep him over in the opposite direction using the next technique in this section. With most MMA fighters now possessing excellent sweep defense, you often need to go from one sweep to another until you manage to get one step ahead of him.

I'm sitting up in the butterfly guard. I've established a left under-hook on Albert, and I'm controlling his left arm by grabbing his triceps with my right hand.

As I fall to my right side, I do several things at once. I elevate Albert's right hip using my left butterfly hook, I carry his body down with me using my left under-hook, and I use my right arm to trap his left arm to my side, which prevents him from countering the sweep by posting his left hand on the mat.

I continue to roll over to my right side, lifting Albert's hips with my left butterfly hook and pulling him over with me using my left under-hook.

Still driving Albert over using my left butterfly hook and left under-hook, I push off my right leg and turn my hips over in a counterclockwise direction.

Using my left under-hook to stay tight to Albert's body, I sweep him all the way over to his back.

Dropping my weight down on top of Albert, I shift my hips so that my left hip is flat to the ground. To secure side control, I keep my left arm hooked underneath his right arm for control and pull his left arm up using my right hand. This last action not only helps me drive my weight down into him to avoid a scramble, but it also hinders him from wedging his arm to the inside of my hips.

BUTTERFLY SWEEP (OPTION 2)

When you execute the previous butterfly sweep and your opponent counters by posting his leg, a good option is to hook your arm underneath his leg and sweep him over in the opposite direction. However, in order to be successful with this technique there can be no hesitation. You must flow directly from the previous sweep into this technique, making it one fluid motion. If your opponent counters this second option, you may want to flow back into the original sweep or abort the sequence altogether and work back to your feet. Deciding what to do will depend upon the openings your movement creates.

I'm sitting up in the butterfly guard. I've established a left under-hook on Albert, and I'm controlling his left arm by grabbing his triceps with my right hand.

As I fall to my right side, I do several things at once. I elevate Albert's right hip using my left butterfly hook, I carry his body down with me using my left under-hook, and I use my right arm to trap his left arm to my side, which prevents him from countering the sweep by posting his left hand on the mat.

Unable to block the sweep by posting his left arm, Albert counters by posting his left leg out.

The instant Albert posts out on his left leg, I swoop my right arm underneath his leg and establish an under-hook.

To sweep Albert in the opposite direction, I turn to my left side, elevate his hips by kicking my left leg out, and driving his left leg off the mat using my right under-hook.

Continuing to force Albert over to his back using my right under-hook on his left leg, I drop my left leg to the mat, push off my right foot, and begin to turn into him.

As Albert is forced onto his back, I follow him over. To secure the side control position, I drive my weight down into him, flatten my hips out on the mat, and bring my right knee up to his left hip.

HALF GUARD

Half Guard Top

When I establish the top half-guard position, my primary goal is to transition all the way to the mount. Sometimes I'll use straight-up jiu-jitsu to achieve this goal, and sometimes I'll soften my opponent up with strikes to make the transition easier to manage. If you choose the latter option, it is important not to get so caught up with landing devastating strikes that you compromise your positioning and let your opponent escape to full guard or sweep you over to your back. Although you have a lot of options from half-guard, you must always concentrate on maintaining control of your opponent. Obtaining that control isn't difficult. If your opponent has your right leg trapped between his legs, you'll want to secure an under-hook with your right arm and keep your opponent pinned flat on his back to neutralize his offense. As long as you can maintain that control, you'll be able to safely set up your pass into mount or side control. Just don't stay in half-guard all day long. You most likely had to do some work to achieve half-guard (either getting the takedown or freeing one leg from your opponent's guard), so work on getting the pass. The longer you wait, the more chances you give your opponent to escape.

Key Concepts for Half Guard Top

✓ Just as you do in full guard; use your strikes to set up passes and your passes to set up strikes.
✓ To prevent your opponent from attacking with sweeps, work to pin him flat to the mat.

Half Guard Bottom

If you're in the bottom half-guard position and your opponent is an expert working from the top half-guard position, you could end up in some trouble. He has a whole bunch of strikes at his disposal, and you don't have many. For this reason, it is imperative that you quickly assess what moves are available to you and then go for them. You don't want to hang out and burn time. When I find myself in the bottom half-guard position, I'll work to establish an under-hook and then get up onto my side. Once achieved, I'll work to take my opponent's back or sweep him over to his back. You should feel a sense of urgency. Assess your situation, force movement, and get out of there. Trying to stall in the bottom half-guard position will most likely cause you some pain.

Key Concepts for Half Guard Bottom

✓ Get onto your side and establish an under-hook. If your left leg is trapped, you want to get up to your left side and establish a left under-hook.
✓ Immediately work your sweeps when end up in the bottom half-guard position.
✓ Keeping moving back and forth until you manage a sweep. Constant movement keeps your opponent off balance, making it difficult for him to strike and pass.

GRINDING ELBOW FROM HALF GUARD

Throwing elbow strikes from the top half-guard position is an excellent way to open a cut. For the best results, you want to drop your weight into the strike and then grind the tip of your elbow in or around your opponent's eye socket. The nice part about this attack is that you can pop up, pin your opponent's head to the mat, smash an elbow into his face, and then quickly drop back down and regain control.

I'm postured up in Reagan's half-guard, driving his head into the mat with my left hand.

Distributing my weight over my left arm, I let my hand slip forward and then drop all of my weight downward, crashing the tip of my elbow just underneath Reagan's left eye.

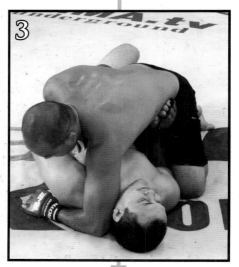

Continuing to drive my weight downward, I grind my elbow down the left side of Reagan's face.

NO-HAND PASS TO MOUNT

This is probably the best pass that you can utilize from half-guard. It takes you directly to the mount, and because you have control of your opponent's head and one of his arms, it makes it very difficult for him to rabbit punch you in the face as you make the transition. However, there are a few key things you should remember when performing this pass. You want to keep your head down in order to maintain a solid base, and you want to get your hips high because it will cause your opponent's grip on your leg to slip. This is especially true if it's deep in the fight and both of you are slippery with sweat. Once you get your foot out, you can head to the mount as I show below, or you can transition to side control, which is the next technique in the section. Deciding which technique to choose will depend upon your opponent's resistance.

1

I'm in Albert's half guard. I've got a right under-hook, my left arm is wrapped underneath his head, my hands are clasped together under his left shoulder, and I'm driving my weight down into him.

2

Pushing off my right foot, I get my head to the mat and drive my left shoulder into Albert's face. I then lift my hips in the air and maneuver my left foot to the inside of Albert's right knee.

3

I continue to elevate my hips and drive my left shoulder into Albert's face. As I do this, I pry his legs open by forcing my left leg to the mat.

4

Pinning Albert's right leg to the mat with my left leg, I begin to wedge my right knee over his left thigh and make my transition to mount. It is important to notice that I am still driving my weight forward with my head on the ground. This not only keeps Albert pinned to the mat, but it also gives me a sturdy base as I make the transition.

I slide my right leg over Albert's left leg, and I slide my left leg over Albert's right leg. Immediately I drop both legs to the mat to eliminate space, making it very difficult for Albert to put me back into his half guard.

To secure the mount, I bring my heels together underneath Albert's legs.

THE GROUND GAME

No-Hand Pass to Side Control

Although I personally like to utilize the no-hand pass to transition from half guard into the mount, it doesn't mean that using the pass to move into side control isn't a good option. If your opponent is blocking the mount or your mount is weak and you're an expert at delivering strikes from side control, you'll probably want to transition into side control. But you should still learn how to make both transitions. Every time the no-hand pass becomes available, you'll be surrounded by a different set of variables. You have to take into consideration the strengths and weaknesses of your opponent. You have to take into consideration the openings he is offering you. If you become just as proficient working from side control as you are from the mount, the passing technique you choose to utilize will be based less on your personal limitations and more on the situation at hand.

1

I'm in Albert's half guard. I've got a right under-hook, my left arm is wrapped underneath his head, my hands are clasped together under his left shoulder, and I'm driving my weight down into him.

2

Pushing off my right foot, I get my head to the mat and drive my left shoulder into Albert's face. I then lift my hips in the air and maneuver my left foot to the inside of Albert's right knee.

I continue to elevate my hips and drive my left shoulder into Albert's face. As I do this, I pry his legs open by forcing my left leg to the mat. Instead of wedging my right knee over Albert's left leg as I did in the previous technique, I turn my hips in a clockwise direction and wedge my right knee underneath my left leg. It is importance to notice that I'm maintaining my base during the transition by keeping my weight forward and driving my left shoulder into Albert's face.

4

I slide my right leg down to the mat on Albert's right side. Once my right leg is clear, I secure side control by stepping out with my left leg and flattening my hips to the mat.

GETTING THE UNDER-HOOK FROM HALF GUARD

When you find yourself in the bottom half-guard position, your opponent will usually do one of two things. Either he will posture up so he can rain down strikes or he will keep his weight pressed down on top of you to prevent you from moving. This technique should be utilized when your opponent drops his weight down on top of you. If he has his arms underneath your arms, there is very little you can do in the way of offense. However, if you can get up onto one side and establish an under-hook, you gain the ability to sweep your opponent or transition to his back. To get the under-hook, you will need to use your hips to create separation between your body and your opponent's body. Once you get that separation, slipping your arm underneath your opponent's arm becomes quite easy. If your opponent willingly gives you that space so he can posture up and strike, then you'll want to sit up into him and establish an under-hook as I do in the following technique.

Beach is on top of me in my half guard, pinning my back to the mat. In order to get offensive, I must create separation between us and establish an under-hook on my left side. If you have your opponent's left leg trapped, then you'll want to establish an under-hook on your right side.

I create distance by cranking my hips to my right and getting onto my right side.

Bringing my left arm up over Beach's head, I prepare to drive my arm into the gap I created between our bodies.

I drive my left arm between our chests and begin to wedge it underneath Beach's right arm to establish an under-hook.

I sweep my left arm under Beach's body and right arm, and then wrap it around his back to secure a left under-hook.

HALF GUARD TO BACK

Although this is a very simple transition that is easy to defend against, it's usually the first technique I'll attempt from the bottom half-guard position. Unless I'm up against a complete amateur, I don't expect to pull this move off; I expect my opponent to block the transition by clamping down on my arm with an over-hook and driving his weight into me. The reason I still execute this technique is because my opponent's defense sets me up to sweep him in the opposite direction using the next technique in this section. If you don't attempt to take your opponent's back with this technique, you won't get the sweep that follows. To increase your chances of being successful with this sweep, you want to rock backward before trying to take your opponent's back. You do this because it pulls your opponent's weight forward and forces him to base out on his hands. This often gives you that extra little space needed to successfully slip out from underneath him.

Beach is postured up in my half guard.

As I sit up, I reach my left arm underneath Beach's right arm to establish an under-hook. At the same time, I maneuver my right arm to the inside of Beach's left leg. It is important to notice how tight I am to Beach. In order to prevent your opponent from blocking your transition, you want to keep your head tight to him and close all distance between your bodies.

I reach my left arm around the back of Beach's right leg and pull his base forward. I then rock onto my right side and begin to maneuver my left leg over Beach's right leg.

I hook my left leg over Beach's right leg, and then I coil my left leg back while controlling his hips with my arms.

Posting on my right elbow and using my under-hook to throw off Beach's base, I slip my body out from underneath him.

Beach could have countered my transition to his back by throwing his right arm over my left arm and clamping down with a whizzer, but he failed to do so. As a result, I come up onto my right knee and continue my transition to his back. It is important to notice that my right leg is laced under Beach's right leg. This gives me one hook. To secure the back position, all I have to do is throw my left leg over his back and secure my second hook.

To secure the back position, I throw my left leg over Beach's body and slide it to the inside of his left leg. Clamping down, I prepare to launch my assault.

HALF GUARD REVERSE SWEEP

This sweep becomes available when you attempt to take your opponent's back from the bottom half-guard position and he counters by clamping down on your arm with a whizzer and driving his weight into you. As your opponent does this, he creates a lot of downward momentum, and you want to use that momentum against him by immediately sweeping him over to his back and obtaining side control. I can't emphasis enough how fluid you need to be with this transition. The moment your opponent drives his weight down, you want use your under-hook on his leg to help power him over. If your opponent has a chance to stop his momentum, you won't get the sweep. When you run into such a scenario, you might want to try sweeping him in the opposite direction. If he defends that sweep, you're once again set up for the sweep below. Because you're in such a low half-guard position, you can often see-saw back and forth between the two techniques until you manage to pull one off.

Here I'm working to take Beach's back just as I did in the previous technique. I've hooked my right arm deep around the inside of his left leg, reached my left arm around the back of his right leg and pulled his base forward, rolled onto my right side, hooked my left leg over his right leg, and coiled my left leg back.

Posting on my right elbow, I use my under-hook to throw off Beach's base, and then I slip my body out from underneath him. Before I can take Beach's back, he blocks my transition by establishing a tight over-hook on my left arm and driving his weight down into me.

As soon as I feel resistance, I fall down to my right side and use Beach's downward momentum against him by rolling to my left. As I roll, I coil my left leg back, pull on his right leg with my left arm, and drive my right under-hook upwards.

I continue to force Beach over to his back by driving my under-hook over the top, as well as pulling on his right leg with my left leg and left arm.

Continuing to drive off my right foot, I follow Beach all the way over.

To secure side control, I bring my knees tight to Beach's body and flatten my hips to the mat.

SIDE CONTROL

Side Control Top

There are two different top side-control positions that I tend to utilize. The first is standard side control. To achieve this position you want to lie on top of your opponent with your body perpendicular to his. Press your weight down into his torso, keep your hips low to the ground, and use your arms to control him. Although you can land some devastating knee strikes from here, you can't do too much in the punching department because both of your arms are tied up with keeping your opponent trapped beneath you. The main benefit of standard side control is your ability to effectively transition into the mount.

The second position I utilize is a modified side control. In order to open up my striking options, I'll switch my base by turning my hips toward my opponent's head. When you do this, it allows you to control your opponent by leaning your weight into him. With your hands freed up, you can land an assortment of punches and elbow strikes to your opponent's face. The downside to modified side-control is that your ability to move is limited, making a transition to the mount hard to manage.

Unless your opponent is completely gassed, you shouldn't expect him to just lie on his back and let you work. He will snap his hips and do everything he can think of to escape the bottom side control position. A good way to prevent him from achieving his goal is to switch back and forth between the two side-control positions I described above. When you want to land some strikes, turn your hips toward his head and lean your weight into him. When you want mobility, flatten your hips to the ground.

Although a lot of fighters like to work from side control because they feel they can't get bridged or turned over, I personally like to soften my opponent up with a couple of strikes and then either lock in a submission or make the transition to the mount or back, both of which I feel are much more secure positions. You just can't generate the same kind of power behind your punches from side control as you can from the mount, and if you can't cause any damage to your opponent, it's only a matter of time until the referee stands the fight back up. You've got to continuously be moving and forcing movement out of your opponent. Work your ground and pound, and work to take your opponent's back or climb into mount. Just keep forcing movement until your opponent makes a mistake that results in your victory.

Key Concepts for Side Control

✓Always establish the side-control position before working for strikes or submissions.
✓Standard side control is best suited for transitioning to the mount.
✓Turning your torso toward your opponent's head opens up more striking and submission options, but it restricts your movement, making the transition to the mount difficult.
✓Drive your weight into your opponent to control his movement.
✓To prevent your opponent from escaping back to his feet, always be setting up your next transition, strike, or submission.

Side Control Escapes

When stuck in the bottom side-control position, you never want to turn away from your opponent because it exposes your back. You want to turn into him. The positioning of your arms is also very important. If your opponent has his legs on your left side, you want to keep your left arm up to protect your head from devastating strikes, and you want to keep your right arm draped across your torso so you can push on your opponent to get to your side, create separation, and work for an escape. If your opponent manages to put you flat on your back, you're in a bad spot. You'll be forced to fight and defend exclusively with your arms, which gets exhausting. But even when you manage to obtain good posture and angle into your opponent, you still need to get out of there as quickly as possible. Your opponent will most likely unleash with strikes, go for submissions, and try to climb into mount or take your back. Just like when you're in the bottom half-guard position, you need to have a sense of urgency, except here that sense of urgency needs to be even greater. Ideally you want to bridge your opponent off the top position or create space between you and your opponent and get back to your knees. You can also work to pull your opponent into your guard. Nothing good will happen for you as long as you're in the bottom side-control position, so you must do what it takes to escape.

BEAT DOWN POSITION

As I mentioned in the introduction, the standard side-control position isn't optimal for striking because you're using your arms to maintain control of your opponent. However, transitioning to the beat down position opens up your striking options big time. To obtain this position, you want to force your opponent's near arm to the mat with your hand, and then trap it there by planting your knee on top of it. As long as you can maintain control of your opponent's far arm using your far arm and head, your opponent's face will be left unprotected, allowing you to drop an assortment of downward strikes with your free arm. Once you've achieved this positioning, your opponent is in serious trouble. It's still possible for him to escape, but he's going to have to use a considerable amount of energy to do so. Just keep dropping bombs until you knock your opponent out or the referee puts a stop to the abuse.

I'm in the side control position. My left arm is wrapped around Troy's head, and my right arm is hooked underneath his left arm. Troy has his arms locked around my back to prevent me from striking.

Unhooking my hands, I pull my left arm out from underneath Troy's head and place my forearm on the right side of his face.

I drive the sharp part of my wrist down into Troy's jaw, forcing his head to the left. My action forces his hands apart.

Having broken Troy's grip, I post my left foot back and come up onto my right hip. This allows me to wedge my left arm to the inside of Troy's right arm.

Pinning Troy's right arm to the mat using my left hand, I wedge my left knee underneath my left arm.

I trap Troy's right arm to the mat using my left shin. Notice how I plant my left knee on the mat above his right biceps.

Keeping Troy's left arm wedged against my neck, I cup my right hand over his left shoulder. With his left arm trapped, I lift my left arm and prepare to drop an elbow to his face.

I drop a hard elbow into Troy's face.

Troy can do little to protect his face, so I cock my left hand back to land another strike.

This time I drop my left fist into Troy's face. I will continue dropping a barrage of downward strikes until Troy taps or the referee stops the fight.

DOWNWARD GRINDING ELBOW

The downward grinding elbow is one of the few strikes that you can land from standard side control. To execute this move, you want to pin your opponent's far arm to the mat with your hand closest to his legs, and then drive your opposite elbow down into his face. Although the move looks rather simple, it can be a little tricky learning how to make the most of your weight. You want to position yourself so that you're not only using your weight to pin your opponent's arm, but also to generate power behind your strike. As with all strikes, it is important that you execute the technique quickly. You want to pop up, and then instantly drop your elbow.

I've secured the top side control position.

I reach my right arm over Butch's body and then pin his left arm to the mat with my right hand. To prevent him from turning into me, I slide my right knee up to his right hip.

I grip Butch's left biceps with my right hand so that my thumb is facing away from my body. To pin his arm to the mat, I come up onto my right knee, post on my left foot, and straighten my right arm. As I do this, I plant my left hand on Butch's face and prepare to drop a left elbow.

Pressing down with my left arm, I let my hand slip off the side of Butch's face and collapse my elbow. I drop my weight as my arm collapses, and the tip of my left elbow crashes into Butch's right eye.

As I rake my elbow down the side of Butch's face, I let my weight fall to the mat, putting me back into standard side control.

KNEE TO SIDE

Throwing knee strikes to your opponent's body from the top side-control position probably won't win you the fight, but they can wear your opponent down and rack up some points on the judges' scorecards. To execute this technique, you want to come up onto the knee closest to your opponent's head and extend your other leg straight back. As you quickly drive your knee toward your opponent's ribs, you want to brace his body with both arms to ensure he absorbs the full brunt of the blow. Once you've landed a few shots, go for a submission, make your transition to the mount, or shift your base so you can land some punches and elbows. Although it is possible to remain in this position, landing one knee strike after another, your opponent will most likely move while under fire, giving you better options.

I'm in standard side control.

As I come up onto my left knee, I throw my right leg straight back.

Bending my right knee to make it as sharp as possible, I drive it forward into Butch's right side.

I drop my hips and reset my base.

KNEE TO HEAD

Landing a knee to your opponent's head from the top side-control position is a great option if the event you're competing in allows it. If it lands, there is a high probability that the fight will come to a dramatic end. At the very least, your opponent will be fazed. The mechanics of this technique are similar to landing a knee to your opponent's body, except here you are striking with the knee closest to his head. It is important to notice how I drive my head forward and to the ground for the attack. This allows me to maintain my base and keep my weight over the top of my opponent as I strike. It is also key to notice that I post my left arm next to my opponent's head. This limits the mobility of his head, which ensures that he absorbs the full impact of the knee. To get the most out of this technique, you want to get your hips and leg high off the ground and then drive all of your weight downward.

I'm in standard side control.

Placing my right knee against Butch's right hip, I elevate my hips by coming up onto my right knee and left foot. As I drive my weight forward and get my head to the mat, I press my left arm against the left side of Butch's head to trap it in place.

Still pressing my weight forward, I lift my left leg straight into the air.

Bending my left leg to make it as sharp as possible, I drive my knee into the side of Butch's face.

Dropping my hips flat to the mat, I reestablish my base.

KNEES TO HEAD (OPTION 2)

This knee strike comes in handy from the top side-control position when your opponent uses his near arm to protect himself from the previous knee strike, which comes straight in at his head. To get past your opponent's guard, you want to switch your base so that your hips are facing his head, and then slide the leg you still have on the mat underneath your elevated leg. If you look at the photos below, you will notice how this prevents your opponent from posting his arm on the leg you're attacking with. This allows you to bring your attacking leg up and over your opponent's arm, and then down to his face.

I'm in side control.

Posting on my left leg, I switch my base by sliding my right leg underneath my left.

I straighten my right leg as I slide it out from underneath my left leg. To switch my base completely, I step my left leg further back. With my hips facing Paco's head, I cup the left side of his face with my left hand and keep my right elbow wedged tight against his left hip.

Pushing off my right leg, I lift my left leg off the mat.

Turning my hips over, I bring my left knee over the top and then angle it down toward Paco's face.

Rotating my hips all the way over, I crash my left knee into Paco's jaw.

I step my left foot behind my right leg to reestablish my base.

STRIKING TO AMERICANA

To execute this technique you first need to put yourself in a position to strike, and this can be managed by turning your hips toward your opponent's head and then walking your leg over his near arm to trap it to the mat. Once you achieve this, you can start dropping hammer fists and elbows to your opponent's unprotected face. He won't be able to defend the shots with his near arm as long as it's stuck to the mat, so he will most likely attempt to guard his face with his far arm. The moment he does this, it allows you to snatch up his far arm, pin it to the mat, and finish the fight with the Americana submission.

I'm in the modified side control with my back facing Paco's legs. My right elbow is pressed securely against his left hip and my legs are flared out to maintain my base. It is important to position your weight directly over your opponent to prevent him from scrambling.

I slide my left arm to the inside of Paco's right arm, and then I force his arm between my legs.

Holding Paco's right arm down with my left hand, I step my left leg over his arm.

I trap Paco's left arm by stepping my leg over the top of it and then coiling my leg back. Notice how this pinches his arm behind my left knee.

With Paco's right arm out of the picture, I lift my left arm to drop a hammer fist to his unprotected face.

I smash a hammer fist into Paco's nose.

As Paco maneuvers his left arm up to protect his face, I place my left hand on his wrist and begin forcing his arm to the mat.

I switch my base by flattening my hips out on the mat. This allows me to use my weight to pin Paco's left arm down on the top of my right arm.

I grip my left wrist with my right hand and then pull Paco's left arm tight to our bodies (this is a necessary step because it gives me the leverage to lock in the hold). To finish the submission, I press down on Paco's wrist with my left hand, and pull his elbow up with my right arm.

STRIKING TO KIMURA

If your opponent is a good jiu-jitsu player and you trap him in the bottom side-control position, he will most likely make it very difficult for you to climb into the mount or land hard strikes. He'll have his near arm up to protect his head from knee strikes, and he'll have his far arm draped across his torso so he can push on your body and create separation. However, anytime your opponent has his arm draped across his body, he is giving you an opportunity to lock in a Kimura. To set up the submission, grab his wrist with your arm closest to his legs and then turn your hips so that your back is facing his head. The goal is to force his arm down to the mat, but if your opponent defends by grabbing onto his shorts or gripping the inside of his thigh, a good option is to land some hard elbows to the side of his unprotected head. As soon as your opponent loosens his grip, you can return to the Kimura and work to finish the submission. Constantly going back and forth between the Kimura and striking greatly increases your chances of finishing your opponent.

I'm in the side control position.

Latching onto Paco's left wrist with my right hand, I begin to switch my base by bringing my left leg underneath my right leg. This turns my hips toward Paco's legs.

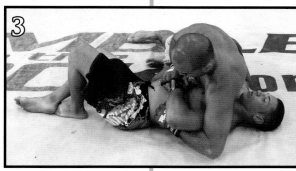

Bringing my left leg all the way underneath my right leg so that my hips are facing Paco's legs, I scoop my left arm underneath his left arm to lock in the Kimura.

As I slide my left arm underneath Paco's left arm, his focus shifts to defending against the Kimura. I take the opportunity to jam my left elbow straight back into his face.

The instant I land the elbow, Paco's focus returns to defending against my strikes. I use the opportunity to quickly slip my left arm back underneath his left arm.

I latch onto my right wrist with my left hand. Then I switch my base back to standard side control by sliding my left leg underneath my right.

Still grabbing my right wrist with my left hand, I step my left leg over Paco's right arm and head.

Pushing off the mat with my left foot, I pull Paco off the ground using the Kimura lock. I then pull my left arm in and push my right hand to my left. By turning my arms in a counterclockwise direction, I finish the Kimura and put a great amount of pressure on Paco's left shoulder.

STANDARD SIDE CONTROL TO MOUNT

Although this is a very simple way to transition from the top side-control position into the mount, everyone entering MMA competition should have this technique in their arsenal. To execute this move, you want to establish tight head and arm control, plant your knee on your opponent's belly, and then drag your leg over to the other side.

I'm in standard side control. I've established an over-under body-lock by sliding my left arm underneath Paco's head, hooking my right arm underneath his left arm, and then clasping my hands together underneath his left shoulder.

To begin my transition to the mount, I post on my left foot, elevate my hips, and begin driving my right knee across Paco's belly. It is important to notice that I am driving my weight down through my shoulders to keep Paco pinned to the mat.

Pressing my weight forward, I slide my right knee down to the mat on Paco's left side.

I drop my right leg down to the mat on Paco's left side.

To secure the mount, I bring my heels together underneath Paco's legs.

STEPPING OVER TO MOUNT

In the previous technique you placed your knee on your opponent's belly and slid your way over into the mount. When your opponent prevents you from doing this by crossing his legs, this is an excellent technique to employ. To pull it off, all you have to do is switch your base so that your hips are facing your opponent's legs, pull his elevated knee down using your hand, and then step your leg over the top of your opponent to establish the mount position.

I'm in side control with my hips facing Paco's legs.

I lift my left arm and place my hand on Paco's right knee.

Pushing Paco's right leg toward the mat on his left side, I begin stepping my left leg over his body.

Clearing my left leg over Paco's body, I bring my left knee down to the mat on his right side. To secure the mount, I touch my heels together under his legs and bring my right arm to the left side of his head.

THE GROUND GAME

ATTACKING FROM KNEE ON BELLY

If your opponent is a really good jiu-jitsu player, it can sometimes be difficult to land strikes or mount him from the top side-control position. In such a situation, it's only a matter of time until the referee stands the fight back up due to inactivity. If you want to keep your dominant positioning, forcing movement is critical. A good way to achieve this is to transition to the knee on belly position. Once there, you have a lot of mobility. You can land strikes, hop over your opponent, or walk around his head as he turns into you to escape. Whichever option you choose, your opponent will be forced to scramble, which keeps the referee happy and the fight on the ground. If at anytime you feel in danger of losing your positioning, you can simply drop back down into the standard side control position.

I'm in standard side control.

I plant my right hand on Paco's belly and my left hand on his neck. I then push off with both hands to increase my elevation.

As I fully extend my arms, I get the separation needed to slide my right knee across Paco's belly.

I cock my right hand back.

I throw my right hand into Paco's jaw.

As I come down with a left handed strike, Paco covers up and turns into me.

The moment Paco turns into me, I plant my hands on his chest and jump over his body to establish knee on belly control on his left side.

I establish knee and belly control on Paco's left side.

I cock my right hand back to continue with my assault.

I smash my right hand through Paco's guard.

I sneak a left hand through Paco's guard.

12

Paco rolls to his left to turn into me. Instead of jumping over his body, I step my right leg forward and begin to circle around his head.

13

Coming up onto both feet, I continue to circle around Paco's head in a counterclockwise direction.

14

I've circled all the way around Paco's head to the right side of his body. Even though I'm standing, notice how little space there is between Paco's body and my legs. It is important that you maintain constant contact with your opponent as you fight to regain control.

15

Pressing all my weight through my right leg and into Paco's right side, I drop my level and prepare to reassume side control.

16

Dropping down to both knees, I slide my left arm underneath Paco's head and my right arm underneath his right arm. From here, I can work to take Paco's back or reestablish the side control position.

ESCAPE TO GUARD FROM SIDE CONTROL BOTTOM

This technique is a basic jiu-jitsu escape that takes you from the bottom side control position to full guard. All you're doing in this move is creating separation by scooting your hips out, and then sliding your knee between your body and your opponent's body to capture him between your legs. It's much better to escape to a top position or climb back to your feet, but getting to guard is much easier to accomplish. Once you've got your opponent in your guard, you have a lot more options at your disposal than you do from the bottom side-control position.

I'm stuck in the bottom side control position.

Pushing off my posted left leg, I scoot my hips back to create the separation I need to slide my right leg in front of Paco's legs. As I do this, I push on Paco's hips with both of my hands to prevent him from closing the gap I just created.

I jam my right leg in front of Paco's hips.

As I pull my right knee out from underneath Paco on his left side, I square my hips up with his body and hook my left leg over his back.

I scoot my hips to my right. This creates enough space to inch my entire right leg out from underneath Paco's body.

I capture Paco in my closed guard by wrapping my right leg over his back and hooking my left foot under my right foot. To control his posture, I wrap my left arm around the back of his head.

THE GROUND GAME

GET UP ESCAPE FROM SIDE CONTROL BOTTOM

This technique allows you to escape up to your feet when stuck in the bottom side control position. Although pulling guard is easier, this is usually the better option because you're no longer stuck on your back.

I'm stuck in the bottom side control position.

Pushing on Paco's hips with both hands, I circle my hips out in a counterclockwise direction.

Continuing to circle my hips around in a counterclockwise direction, I rotate my body over so that I'm belly-down on the mat. To prevent Paco from running around and taking my back, I'll need to get up to my feet as quickly as possible.

Still pushing off Paco's right hip with my left hand, I get up to my knees.

Posting on my left foot, I stand all the way up.

I push Paco away from me and assume my standard fighting stance.

MOUNT

Top Mount

The mount is my favorite position in MMA because not only do you have your opponent pinned to the mat, but you've also got both of your hands free to throw strikes and go for submissions. I realize that there are a lot of fighters who don't feel the same way. Some fighters fear the mount because they worry about their opponent bridging and putting them on their back. They feel side control is a much safer position to work from. Although their concern is legitimate, it doesn't mean the mount should be ignored. You simply need to master the mount in training. Your goal should be to develop a mount that is stronger than your opponent's escapes. This can be said for all positions. If your passes aren't as strong as your opponent's guard, you're never going to reach side control. In such a situation should you avoid guard altogether? No, you should work on your passes.

With time and practice, your confidence in being able to maintain the mount position will grow. When I fight, I always feel a sense of urgency to obtain the mount, and when I do, I feel an even greater sense of urgency because the end of the fight could be lurking right around the corner. I could end it with strikes, a submission, or by transitioning to my opponent's back and choking him out.

There are three different mount positions that I utilize in MMA competition. The first one I call "mount stabilization control." In this mount you are clinched up with your opponent and have one arm wrapped underneath his head. Because you're pinning your opponent flat on his back, it's an excellent position to stabilize the mount and set up submissions. However, it is not the best position from which to strike.

Neck control is the second mount position I utilize. In this mount, you posture up and pin your opponent's neck to the mat with one hand, making it an excellent position from which to strike. In order to fully capitalize on this mount, it is imperative that you not only learn an assortment of downward strikes, but you also learn what submissions you can execute based upon your opponent's reactions to your strikes.

The third position I use is the double attack mount. It takes a little more to achieve this position, but it's a solid control position that sets you up nicely to strike, execute submissions, or transition to your opponent's back. I give several techniques that you can utilize from each of these three mount positions in the upcoming section, and I suggest you explore all of them. The more tricks you have up your sleeve, the more confident you'll become at obtaining and maintaining the mount position.

Key Concepts for Mount

✓When you transition to the mount, immediately stabilize the position.
✓To stabilize the mount, keep your hips low and press your weight into your opponent. You also want to slide your legs under your opponent's legs and touch your heels together.

Mount Escapes

Other than having an opponent take your back, the bottom mount position is the worst position in MMA. Not only can your opponent land devastating punches, but he can also easily lock in a submission. Escaping should be your primary goal, and you should conserve no energy in the process. Don't rest for even one second. If your opponent pins your neck to the ground, you want to whack his arm away with your hand. If he postures up to land strikes, buck him forward to mess with his balance. Unless you do everything in your power to improve your position, the fight will be over in a flash.

A good way to get better at escaping the bottom mount position is to practice mount drills. One such drill is to have a training partner mount you for one minute. While he throws downward strikes and goes for submissions, your only job is to escape. Every time you get the escape, let your opponent climb back into the mount. It can be quite painful at times, but it's better than getting mounted in a fight and being lost as to how to better your situation.

MOUNT STABILIZATION CONTROL

The first thing you want to do when you reach the mount is stabilize your position. After putting in all that work to get there, you want to make sure that your opponent doesn't escape. To stabilize the mount, drop your weight down on top of your opponent, wrap an arm underneath his head, and drive a shoulder down into his face to cause him some discomfort and limit his mobility. If you have your left hand wrapped around your opponent's head, you can either strike with your right hand or post it on the mat above your opponent's arms to secure your base. Deciding which option to choose depends upon the situation and your opponent's struggle to escape the bottom position. To secure the lower portion of your base, touch your heels together underneath your opponent's legs. If you prefer locking your feet, this can be done also. Once you stabilize the mount, immediately start your offense to see what openings you can create.

I'm in the mount position. Beach has planted his hands on my chest in an attempt to disrupt my base and push me off him.

As Beach drives into my chest with both of his hands, I scoop my right arm to the inside of his left arm.

Pushing my right arm all the way to the ground, I begin slipping my left arm to the inside of Beach's right arm.

258   **THE GROUND GAME**

Punching my left elbow down to the mat, I scoop my left arm underneath Beach's head.

To stabilize the mount, I drive my left shoulder down into Beach's jaw, post my right arm on the mat to maintain my base, and bring my heels together underneath Beach's legs.

BREAKING OVER-UNDER TO NECK CONTROL

When in the mount, you never want to allow your opponent to secure an over-hook and an under-hook because it increases his chances of rolling you over to your back. If your opponent does manage to wrap you up in this manner, you must know how to break his hold and create separation so you can strike and work for submissions. This technique and the one that follows are both excellent ways to accomplish this.

I'm in the mount position. Paco has established an over-hook and an under-hook to prevent me from posturing up.

With Paco using both arms to hang onto me, his left side is exposed. I cock my right arm back to land a punch to his ribs.

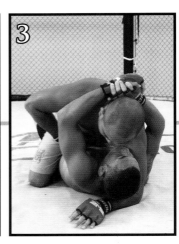

I drop a hard blow to Paco's ribs on his left side.

Instead of drawing my fist back to land another blow, I post my left hand on the mat and elevate my body. This not only forces Paco to support his weight, but it also creates a small gap between our bodies. I punch my right fist through that gap and crash my fist into his jaw.

Turning my right hand over, I place my palm on Paco's face and force his head to the mat, breaking his grip in the process.

I replace my right hand with my left hand and continue to push Paco's head to the mat.

Driving my left hand down into Paco's neck, I posture up and raise my right elbow.

I drop my weight down and land a savage elbow to Paco's face. From here, I can posture back up and throw another downward blow or work for a submission.

BREAKING DOUBLE UNDER-HOOKS

If your opponent establishes double under-hooks when you're in the top mount position, it limits your ability to strike. You can still drive in some rabbit punches, but the hard downward shots are no longer at your disposal. To break the double under-hooks, you want to arch your back, sit up, and then push your opponent's head down to the mat with one hand. Just make sure you don't sacrifice your base. Once you've created that space, you can once again start doing some damage with strikes.

I'm in the mount position. Paco has wrapped both arms around my back to prevent me from posturing up.

Posting on my left hand, I sit up and arch my back. As I come up, I wedge my right hand over Paco's face and begin driving it to the mat.

I break Paco's grip by forcing his head to the mat with my right hand.

I replace my right hand with my left hand and continue to drive Paco's head into the mat.

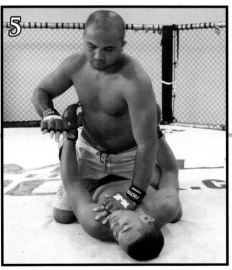

Driving my left hand into Paco's neck, I cock my right arm back.

Dropping my weight, I drop a vicious over-the-top elbow to Paco's face.

STRIKING FROM NECK CONTROL

If your opponent constantly moves his head from side to side, it can be difficult to punch him in the face from the top mount position. In such a scenario, I like to C-cup his neck with one hand and then straighten my arm. In addition to holding his head in place, it also cuts off his air supply. Below I demonstrate how to deliver the hammer fist, the elbow, and the straight right from this position. Although these tend to be the most damaging strikes, you should play around to see what you like best. The main thing you need to focus on when striking from this position is maintaining your base. Your opponent isn't just going to lie there; he is going to snap! You must be ready to counter his scramble by reestablishing the position, transitioning to his back, or locking in a submission.

I'm in the mount position. Opening my left hand, I drive the 'V' between my thumb and fingers into Beach's neck. To strangle him, I lock my left arm and drive my weight straight down into his neck.

I cock my right hand back to drop a hammer fist to Beach's face.

Keeping Beach's head pinned to the mat with my left hand, I drop a hammer fist into his left eye.

I cock my right hand back to come down with another strike.

Dropping my weight, I throw an over-the-top elbow into Beach's face. The tip of my elbow lands in his left eye.

I draw my right hand back again.

This time I throw a right punch, once again targeting Beach's left eye.

STRIKING TO ARM BAR

Most fighters know not to straighten their arms upward when in the bottom mount position. However, when you establish neck control and begin raining down punches at your opponent's face, there is a good chance that he will forget this cardinal rule and straighten his arms to either block your strikes or push you off him. The moment he does this, you have an opening to quickly transition to an arm bar and finish the fight.

I'm in the mount position. Opening my left hand, I drive the 'V' between my thumb and fingers into Beach's neck. To strangle him, I lock my left arm straight and drive my weight down into his neck.

I cock my right hand back to drop a punch to Beach's face.

Keeping Beach's head pinned to the mat with my left hand, I drop my fist into his left eye.

As I bring my right hand back to throw another strike, Beach extends both arms in an attempt to block the anticipated blow.

The moment Beach extends his arms, I post my left foot on the mat, rotate my hips in a counterclockwise direction, and drop my right arm to trap his left arm to my chest.

Dropping my weight onto Beach, I step my right leg over his head and sit down on his left shoulder. It is important that when making this transition you get your hips below your opponent's trapped elbow to avoid losing the submission.

As I start to fall down to my back, I wrap my right arm around Beach's left arm to secure it to my chest.

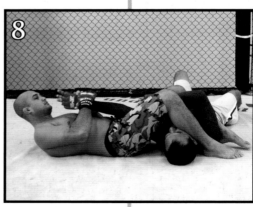

Keeping my legs coiled tight, I fall all the way down to my back and latch onto Beach's left arm with both hands. After making sure Beach's left thumb is pointing toward the ceiling, I finish the submission by squeezing my knees together, pulling his arm toward my chest with both hands, and elevating my hips.

STRIKING TO AMERICANA

When you're in the mount throwing downward punches, your opponent will most likely react in one of three ways. He can extend his arms upward to push you off him, in which case you can catch him in a straight arm bar (p. 263). He can keep his arms tight to his head to block your punches, which allows you to go for an Americana, a kata-gatame choke (p. 267), or establish the double attack position (p. 272). The only other thing he can do is roll over, which allows you to take his back (p. 271). In the sequence below, I'm showing you how to lock in the Americana when your opponent keeps his arms tight to his head.

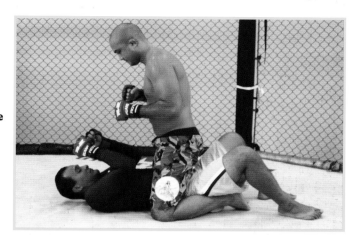

I'm postured up in the mount position.

I drop a straight left hand to Beach's face.

Instead of extending his arms upward, Beach protects his face by keeping his arms in tight. I have the option of working for the kata-gatame choke or the double attack mount, but instead I decide to go for the Americana. I begin by grabbing his right wrist with my right hand immediately after landing the punch.

Pressing my weight forward, I pin Beach's right arm to the mat. Notice how I grind the tip of my right elbow across Beach's face as I drop my right arm down to the mat.

As my right elbow slides off Beach's face and drops to the mat, I slide my left hand underneath his right arm.

Latching onto my right wrist with my left hand, I come up onto my left foot and lean my weight over to my right side to create the angle I need for the submission. To finish the Americana, I push down on Beach's wrist with my right hand and pull his elbow up with my left arm. This puts a tremendous amount of pressure on his shoulder.

MOUNT TO KATA-GATAME ARM TRIANGLE

This is the move that I submitted Duane Ludwig with in K-1 over in Japan. Just like the previous technique, it can be utilized when your opponent keeps his arms pressed tightly against his head to block your downward punches from the mount. Instead of pinning your opponent's arm to the mat, you want to force his arm across his throat and then hold it in place using your head. To ensure he can't escape, you then slip an arm underneath his head and clasp your hands together. After securing your lock, you step out into side control and circle around his head to synch in the choke. It is important to note that if you bail out to side control before your lock is firmly established, your opponent may escape and then you'll have sacrificed your positioning.

I'm postured up in the mount position.

As I draw my right hand back to land a punch to Paco's face, he brings his elbows together and covers up.

Keeping his arms in tight, Paco does a good job defending my strike.

As I cock my right hand back to throw another downward punch, I jam my left hand through Paco's guard and latch onto his neck.

Expecting me to throw another punch, Paco keeps his arms pressed tightly against his head. This creates an opportunity for me to begin pushing his left arm across his neck using my right hand.

As I push Paco's left arm across his neck with my right hand, I press my weight forward and bring my head to the left side of his trapped arm.

I reach my left arm underneath Paco's head and grip my hands together. To trap Paco's left arm across his neck, I drive my weight down into him, squeeze my arms tight, and press my head into his left ear.

Squeezing my arms tight, I step my left leg over Paco's body into the side control position.

To finish the choke, I press my weight into the choke, lay my hips flat on the mat, and squeeze my arms tight.

MOUNTED TRIANGLE

The mounted triangle is easier to get than a lot of fighters think. The important part is not to kamikaze your way through it. You're sitting on top of your opponent, so use your weight to pin him down and set the submission up properly. As long as you can clear your leg over your opponent's arm and figure-four your legs around his head, it doesn't matter if your opponent manages to bridge and roll you over. He's done no matter what.

I'm in the mount. My heels are touching underneath Beach's legs, I'm driving my right shoulder into his face, and I am using my left arm for base.

Scooting my right knee underneath Beach's left shoulder, I lean slightly to my right side and pin his right arm to the mat with my left hand.

Leaning more to my right side, I step my left leg over Beach's trapped arm and plant my foot on the right side of his head. The instant my foot comes down, I latch onto my left instep with my right hand.

Lifting Beach's head with my right arm, I create the space needed to slide my left leg underneath his head.

Shifting my weight to my left side, I bring my right leg forward and hook my left foot behind my right knee.

Once I get my left foot behind my right knee, I coil my right leg back and reset my base.

I pull Beach's left arm up with my right hand.

Using my right hand, I drive Beach's left arm across my body.

To finish the submission, I latch onto Beach's head with both hands and pull up.

MOUNT TO BACK

When you're in the mount throwing all kinds of downward strikes at your opponent's face, it's pretty much a guarantee that he will do everything in his power to escape. A common reaction is that your opponent will roll over onto his stomach to avoid getting hit, in which case you must float on top of him as he rolls underneath you so you can take his back. This requires a lot of sensitivity on your part, and that sensitivity can only come about through hundreds of hours of training. Not having this sensitivity is the reason why a lot of fighters get rolled and lose the mount position. They get so locked into striking that they forget about maintaining their position, and positioning should always be your top priority. When your opponent rolls, forget about strikes for a few seconds, take a portion of your weight off of him so he can roll over to his belly, and then claim his back and start attacking him again with submissions or strikes. If he decides to roll back into you, float on top of him again and reclaim the mount.

I'm postured up in the mount with my right arm cocked back.

I drop a downward elbow to Tony's face.

Not wanting to take more abuse, Tony begins rolling over to his right side. I allow him to roll by slightly lifting my hips off of his body.

As Tony continues to roll over to his belly, I bring my weight back down on the top of him and hook my left arm underneath his left arm, securing an under-hook.

Tony rolls all the way over to his belly. To secure his back, I reach my right arm underneath his right arm, latch onto his right wrist with my right hand, and hook my right leg underneath his right leg to secure my second hook.

DOUBLE ATTACK MOUNT

The double attack mount is an excellent way to put your opponent between a rock and a hard place when he keeps his arms tight to his face to block your downward strikes from the mount. To secure the position, you want to push your opponent's arm across his neck much like you did when going for the kata-gatame arm triangle, except here you are going to lock his arm in place with your body rather than your head. Once you've got his arm locked across his throat, you reach your hand underneath his head, grab hold of his trapped wrist to take his arm completely out of the picture, and then use your control to force him onto his side. I call it the double attack mount because the control position gives you a couple of options. With your opponent on his side, you can attack him from the mount or roll him over and attack him from his back, which I show how to do in the next sequence.

I'm in the mount.

I drop a straight right punch down to Beach's face.

Expecting more punches, Beach locks his arms against his head to protect his face. The moment he does this, I begin pushing his left arm across his neck with my right hand. I also drop my left hand down into his neck and start leaning my weight forward.

I push Beach's left arm across his neck using my right hand, and then I drop my weight on top of his arm to pin it in place.

Keeping my weight pressed forward, I drag my right elbow across Beach's face and post it on the mat to the right of his head.

I drag my right arm across the mat toward the left side of Beach's head. It is very important not to lift your arm off the mat because it will eliminate a portion of your downward pressure and can allow your opponent to pull his trapped arm free. Once I've positioned my right arm on the left side of his head, I begin sliding my arm underneath his head.

Looping my right arm underneath Beach's head, I bring my right knee up and lean slightly to my right side. As I do this, I latch onto Beach's left wrist with my right hand. If you can't reach your opponent's wrist, use your left hand to move his trapped arm closer to your right hand.

Sliding my left arm underneath Beach's left arm, I latch onto my right wrist with my left hand.

Posturing up and posting my left foot on the mat, I pull back with my right hand. This draws Beach's left arm tight around his neck and forces him to roll over onto his right side. I call this the double attack position.

Maintaining a firm grip on Beach's left hand and keeping my left leg snug to his midsection, I pull my left arm free, cock it back, and prepare to drop downward punches.

I blast my left hand into Beach's unprotected face. Although I can land an assortment of strikes from here, I will mostly likely attempt to finish the fight by either taking Beach's back and working for a choke or applying a submission from the mount.

DOUBLE ATTACK TO BACK

Although you can lock in some chokes and perhaps an arm bar from the double attack mount, the position is really designed for taking your opponent's back. Since your opponent's back is already half exposed, all you have to do is sit your opponent up and swing your legs around him to secure back control. Once you've accomplished that, you can immediately start working for the choke.

I'm on top in the double attack position.

Using my arms to lift Beach up into the sitting position, I circle around him in a counterclockwise direction, post on my right knee, and press my weight into his upper back.

Pressing my weight into Beach's upper back to crunch his body forward, I create the space needed to pull my right leg out from underneath my body. Then I begin rolling to my back and swinging my right leg around Beach's right hip.

As I roll onto my back, I pull Beach down with me. To secure the back position, I wrap my right leg around his right hip.

DOUBLE ATTACK TO KATA-GATAME

Once you secure the double attack position, the kata-gatame choke is right there for the taking. Since you already have your opponent's arm trapped across his neck, all you have to do is drop your head to the side of your opponent's arm (using the weight of your body to keep his arm in place), and then step out into side control and finish the fight.

I'm on top of Paco in the double attack position.

I drop my head and place it against Paco's left shoulder. As I pull my right arm out from underneath his head, I begin to slide my left arm underneath his head.

I place my left palm on top of my right palm.

| **THE GROUND GAME**

Locking my hands together, I press my weight forward and begin bailing out into side control.

I step my left leg over Paco's body.

I continue to step my left leg over Paco's legs and transition to side control.

Having stepped out into side control, I drop my hips to the mat, squeeze my arms tight, and press my head into Paco's left shoulder. The idea is to melt your body into the mat and let the pressure of your weight choke your opponent unconscious.

KATA-GATAME CHOKE (ARM TRIANGLE VARIATION)

This technique is similar to the previous one, except here you're using a different grip to choke your opponent unconscious. You still want to trap his arm across his neck and use your weight to pin him down, but rather than stepping all the way out into side control, you lock in an arm triangle and fall to your side. To finish the fight, all you have to do is squeeze your hold tight.

I'm on top of Paco in the double attack position.

Releasing my grip on Paco's wrist, I lift his head up using my right hand. This creates the space I need to slide my left arm deep around his head. It is important to notice that I'm digging the crook of my left elbow into his neck. It is essential that you do this in order for the choke to work.

I latch onto my right biceps with my left hand, and then place my right hand on the top of Paco's head.

Pulling Paco into me, I squeeze my arms together and fall to my right side.

I continue to pull Paco into me as I fall all the way over to my right side. To finish the choke, I squeeze everything tight.

THE GROUND GAME

HIP TO HOLD FROM MOUNT

If your opponent is postured up in the top mount position and he throws a downward strike, bucking your hips is a great way to avoid a damaging strike. As your opponent's body is thrust forward and down, you want to wrap your arms around him. If you can establish a tight hold, it will be difficult for him to throw powerful strikes. Before your opponent can break your hold and posture back up, you want to either work your hips out from under him and escape to guard or secure an over-hook on one of his arms and bridge him over. I demonstrate both of these techniques on the following pages.

Tony is postured up in the mount, preparing to drop a right hand to my face.

As Tony comes down with his punch, I push off both feet and explode my hips upwards.

As Tony's body is cast forward, he posts his hands on the mat. Immediately I sit up, wrap my arms around his back, and grip my hands together.

BASIC BRIDGE ESCAPE

If you plan on entering MMA competition, you need to know the basic bridge escape. It's one of the best techniques to utilize from the bottom mount because you go from one of the worst positions to being on top in your opponent's guard. To execute this move, you want to secure an over-hook on one of your opponent's arms and bridge him to that side. It's also important to secure an under-hook on his opposite side and use that control to help drive him over. Your success rate will depend upon the explosiveness of your bridge and how good your opponent is at holding you down. If you can't bridge your opponent over, then you should immediately resort to the hip-out mount escape, which is the next technique in this section.

Paco is mounted on top of me. It is important to notice that my left arm is under Paco's right arm. This under-hook will help me bridge him over to my right.

Because I've established an under-hook on my left side, I'm going to sweep Paco to my right. To prevent him from blocking the bridge by posting on his left leg, I throw my right leg over his left leg. To prevent him from posting out on his left arm, I pull his left arm tight to my body with my right arm. Then I drive off both feet, punch my left arm upwards, and bridge to my right.

I continue to bridge Paco over to his back.

As Paco is forced to his back, I roll over on top of him, landing in his guard.

I come down onto my knees and secure my base. From here I will work to pass Paco's guard.

HIP-OUT MOUNT ESCAPE

This is another rudimentary way to escape the bottom mount position. Turning onto your side to eliminate some of your opponent's weight from your body, you scoot and pull your legs out from underneath him, and then capture him between your legs in the guard position.

Tony is mounted on top of me. I've established double under-hooks, and I'm gripping my hands together to prevent him from posturing up and pounding me in the face.

I turn onto my right side to elevate Tony's hips and take some of his weight off of me. I then coil my left leg in.

Releasing my grip, I place both hands on Tony's hips and push them down toward my legs. As I do this, I relax my legs and shrimp my hips out from between his legs.

THE GROUND GAME

Continuing to shrimp my body, I pull my hips and legs out from underneath Tony.

Once my legs are free, I roll to my back, spin in a clockwise direction to square my body up with Tony's body, and place my left foot on his right hip.

I complete my transition to open guard by placing my right foot on Tony's left hip.

RUNNING UP THE CAGE MOUNT ESCAPE

If you should find yourself mounted near the cage, this technique can provide a quick escape. All you're doing is walking your feet up the chain link, and then bridging and kicking off the cage to put your opponent onto his back. The only difference between this technique and the normal bridge escape is that you're getting extra elevation to make your escape easier to manage.

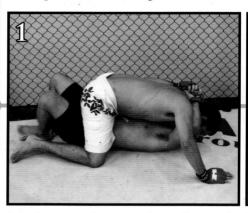

Tony is mounted on top of me. I've established an over-hook and an under-hook, and I'm gripping my hands together to prevent him from posturing up and pounding me in the face. This lock is very important to maintain if you want a technique like this one to work. If you allow your opponent to posture up or base his arms out to his sides, you're going to have a rough time bridging him over.

I place my right foot up on the cage.

I explode off my left leg and thrust my hips upward.

While my momentum is still going upward, I throw my left leg over my right leg and plant my foot high up on the cage.

I blast off the cage with both legs, casting my body over.

My body begins to fall down on top of Tony.

Landing in Tony's guard, I quickly establish my base. From here I will work to pass his guard.

BACK ATTACKS

TURTLE

It's good news when you're able to trap your opponent in the bottom turtle position, but it doesn't mean that you should give up on trying to advance your positioning. A good wrestler can escape the position by standing up, and a good jiu-jitsu practitioner can roll for a knee bar or scramble and pull you into his guard. If your opponent is exhausted and has little fight left, you can milk the position by landing some decent strikes, but if your opponent is fresh, you'll want to attach your chest to his back by establishing an over-under body-lock, hook his closest leg, and then work to secure his back by establishing your second hook. There are a couple of different ways that this can be achieved. You can establish your second hook by rolling to your back and pulling him on top of you, or you can establish your second hook by climbing up onto his back. Both transitions have their place. Deciding which one to employ boils down to the situation and what you're looking to accomplish.

BACK

When you take your opponent's back, there really isn't much that he can do. He has very few options in the offense department, and you have a whole bunch. Your success rate at transitioning to your opponent's back from other positions boils down to how skilled you are in jiu-jitsu, and the only way to acquire good jiu-jitsu skill is to put in the hours on the mat. The back is one of the most dominant positions in the sport, but it is a hard position to acquire, which is why it requires so much attention. In addition to knowing how to reach your opponent's back, you must also understand how to stabilize the position, set up submissions, and strike. The goal is to be able to maintain your position and attack at the same time. If you can't do both simultaneously, it will be difficult to mount an effective offense.

Key Concepts for the Back

✓ When you take your opponent's back, stabilize the position by establishing your hooks. Then work your attacks.
✓ When transitioning to the back from the turtle position, always establish your nearest hook first.
✓ Keep your hips low when you have your opponent's back. If your hips are high, he might be able to buck you off.

BACK ESCAPES

TURTLE

The bottom turtle position is not a place where you want to hang out and take a breather. Your opponent has several options to take your back, and it is also hard to see what your opponent is doing due to your positioning, which means he could land some damaging strikes. And if the event you're competing in allows kicks to a downed opponent, you really have to watch out for your opponent popping up to his feet and kicking you in the head. When you find yourself in the bottom turtle position, you generally want to do one of two things—roll over and capture your opponent in your guard or stand up. I usually prefer the latter.

BACK

When an opponent takes your back, the first thing you must focus on is defending against the choke. There is nothing more important going on in that moment, so it should be your main priority. As you're working to defend against the choke, you should also focus on preventing your opponent from establishing his hooks. If your opponent already has his hooks, then you want to work for an escape by getting your back to the ground, which I demonstrate how to do in the upcoming section.

Key Concepts for Back Escapes

✓ Protect your neck first and foremost.
✓ When stuck in the bottom turtle position, stay balled up to prevent your opponent from establishing his hooks and taking your back.
✓ If your opponent has your back, work to either side of him and get your back flat to the mat. Once you manage this, work to reverse your position by either escaping to guard or rolling over into your opponent's guard.

TURTLE TO BACK SEQUENCE

In the sequence below I demonstrate how to transition from the top turtle position to your opponent's back by establishing a hook on his near leg, rolling to your back, and then pulling him on top of you to establish your second hook. Because this transition can sometimes be difficult using jiu-jitsu alone, I also demonstrate how you can use strikes to soften your opponent up and make the transition easier to manage.

I've secured the turtle position by distributing my weight over Reagan's lower back and wrapping my left arm around his body. Notice that there is very little space between us. This gives me optimal control.

Reagan keeps his right elbow close to his right knee to prevent me from slipping my right foot to the inside of his hip and securing my first hook. Although this makes it difficult to transition to his back, it leaves his face wide open. I capitalize on the opening by crashing my right fist into the side of is head.

Reagan lifts his right arm to protect his head.

The instant Reagan lifts his right arm to protect his head, I thrust my right fist underneath his right arm and catch him in the jaw with an uppercut.

Immediately after I land the uppercut, I pull my right hand out and slide my right foot to the inside of Reagan's right hip, establishing my first hook.

Reaching my right arm around Reagan's head, I drop to my right side and pull him on top of me using my left hand. It is important to note that if your opponent has a solid base, forming an over-under body-lock by gripping your hands together can help you pull your opponent on top of you.

I roll over onto my back and slide my right arm around Reagan's neck. If your opponent is defending his neck, you'll want to establish your second hook before engaging in a hand fight to lock in the choke.

Throwing my left foot over Reagan's left hip, I secure the choke position by bringing my left arm up, latching onto my left biceps with my right hand, and coiling my left arm back so that my left hand is on the top of Reagan's head. To lock in the choke, I squeeze everything tight.

THE BACK |

TURTLE TO BACK SEQUENCE (COUNTERING DEFENSE)

This is the second back transition that you can utilize from the top turtle position. In the previous one, you established a hook on your opponent's near leg, rolled to your back, and then pulled your opponent on top of you so you could get your second hook and start working for a submission. In this sequence, you establish a hook on your opponent's near leg just as before, but then you throw your near leg over your opponent's back to establish your second hook. Once you've got both hooks established, you'll be perched on top of your opponent's back. Ideally you want to use your hooks to flatten your opponent belly-down on the mat to limit his offense, which I show how to do in the next sequence. However, in this sequence your opponent prevents you from flattening him out by quickly standing up. When this happens, utilizing this technique prevents your opponent from climbing all the way up to his feet and shaking you off his back. After nullifying your opponent's escape attempt, he will be forced to retreat back to his knees. From there, you can use your hooks to flatten him belly-down to the mat or pull him on top of you as you did in the previous technique.

I've secured the turtle position by distributing my weight over Reagan's lower back and wrapping my left arm around his body. Notice that there is little space between us. This provides optimal control.

To secure Reagan's back, I need to establish both of my hooks. I get my first hook by wedging my right leg to the inside of Reagan's right hip.

I establish my second hook by stepping my left leg over Reagan's back and wedging my left foot to the inside of his left hip.

Before I can establish the position and flatten Reagan out on the mat, he posts on his arms and begins climbing to his feet.

The moment Reagan posts on his right foot to stand up, I reach my left arm underneath his body and my right arm underneath his right leg. Gripping my hands together, I prevent him from standing up and shaking me off his back.

FLATTENING YOUR OPPONENT

When you utilize the previous technique to take your opponent's back from the top turtle position, flattening him belly-down on the mat should be your main priority. The instant you secure your second hook, you want to drive your weight into your opponent's lower back and sprawl your legs back to force him down to his belly. Once you achieve this, you can go to town with a barrage of punches to the side of his head or work to synch in the choke. When I fought Joey Gilbert early in my UFC career, I used this technique to flatten him out and then hammered away with punches. A few moments later, the referee put an end to the abuse by calling the fight.

I've established back control by hooking both my feet to the inside of Tony's hips.

After securing both hooks, I drive my hips into the small of Tony's back and kick my legs back. This last action pushes Tony's legs out from underneath him and forces him belly-down on the mat.

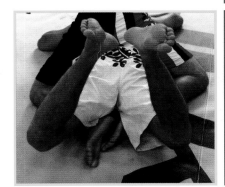

Continuing to drive my hips into Tony's lower back and kick my legs back, I posture up. This applies even more downward pressure to Tony's lower back and flattens him out completely.

Remaining postured up, I drive my right hand into the right side of Tony's head and draw my left hand back for the follow up blow. A good tactic is to bat your opponent's head back and forth between your fists until the referee calls the fight.

KNEEING THE BODY AND HEAD FROM TURTLE

When you reach the top turtle position, your main goal should be to establish your hooks, take your opponent's back, and finish the fight. However, there are times when you might want to deviate from this primary route. If you know your opponent is completely gassed and has no energy left to escape the bottom turtle position, landing powerful knees to his body and head can break his will and possibly even cause the referee to stop the fight. Knee strikes also come in handy when your opponent balls up in the bottom turtle position and keeps his elbows pressed tightly against his legs to prevent you from establishing your first hook. By landing a knee high, you force him to lift his arm to defend his head, which in turn creates the space you need to secure your first hook and take his back.

I'm in the top turtle position on Reagan's right side. I've maneuvered my right hand to the left side of his head; this will give me the leverage I need to really drive my knee strikes forward.

Reagan is guarding his head with his right arm, leaving his right side exposed. To capitalize on the opening, I pull his head toward me with my right hand as I drive my right knee into his ribs.

As I extend my right leg back to land another knee, Reagan drops his right arm to protect his ribs.

By dropping his right arm to protect his ribs, Reagan has exposed his head. As I drive my right knee forward, I pull his head into the strike with my right hand. This not only helps me generate power, but it also prevents him from pulling his head away from the strike and lessening the blow.

REAR NAKED CHOKE FROM BACK

The rear naked choke is the best move ever invented. Once you've got it locked in, you're pretty much guaranteed the victory. However, with most fighters spending lots of time polishing their submission defense, it can sometimes be a difficult submission to lock in. To increase your percentage rate, you might want to try the set-up shown below. If I'm working to slide my left arm around my opponent's neck, I use my right hand to secure my opponent's right arm down by his waist. To defend against the choke, my opponent brings his left arm up. The moment he does this, I use my left hand to shove his left hand down to my side, and then I trap it there by throwing my leg over his arm. With both of my opponent's arms tied up, I cover my opponent's mouth and suffocate him with my left hand. It is certainly possible to submit your opponent this way, but I prefer finishing with the choke because it's a guarantee. To do this, I'll fall to my side and pull my opponent down with me. As soon as our bodies hit the canvas, I wrap my arm underneath his neck and apply the choke.

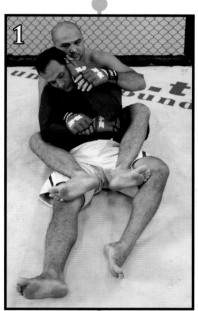

I'm sitting up behind Beach with both hooks established. I have my right arm underneath his right arm, and I'm grabbing onto his right wrist with my right hand (you'll want to maintain this control throughout the duration of the move to prevent your opponent from blocking the choke).

Falling to my right side, I force Beach's left arm down towards my hips with my left hand.

Hooking my left leg over Beach's left arm to trap it down by my hips, I bring my left arm back up and cup my hand over his mouth, suffocating him.

I pull Beach's head to my left side using my left hand. Then I pull back on his head with my left hand and drive my hips into his back. This creates the space I need to wrap my left arm around his neck and secure the choke.

I slide my left arm around Beach's throat and begin falling to my left side.

I drop all the way down to my left side.

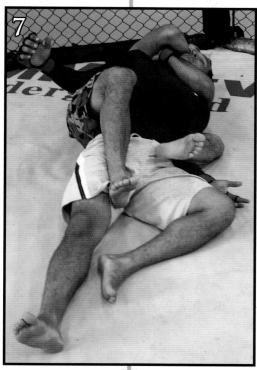

The moment I come down onto my left side, I bring my right arm up, latch onto my right biceps with my left hand, and coil my right arm so that my right hand is behind Beach's head. To secure the choke, I squeeze everything tight.

TRIANGLE ARM BAR FROM BACK

In the previous technique, you used a leg to trap one of your opponent's arms down by your hips to make the rear naked choke easier to manage. When you do this, your opponent might realize his vulnerability and attempt to bridge out and escape. If this should occur, you can slide the leg you're using to trap your opponent's arm up to his shoulder and assume the reverse-triangle position. From there, you can work to finish your opponent with the reverse-triangle submission or go for an arm bar. Most of the time the arm bar is the better option because your opponent rolls right into it.

I have taken Beach's back. I'm sitting up behind him, my right arm is underneath his right arm, I am grabbing his right wrist with my right hand, and I have both hooks established.

As I fall over to my right side, I begin forcing Beach's left arm toward my hips using my left hand.

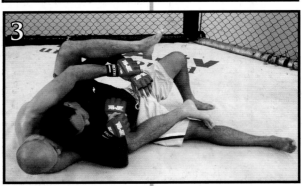

Having forced Beach's left arm down toward my waist, I begin maneuvering my left leg over his left arm.

I maneuver my left leg over Beach's left arm to trap it down by my waist.

Realizing he is in a vulnerable spot, Beach tries to escape by rolling out to his right. As he does this, I bring my left leg up onto his left shoulder. It is very important that you constantly maintain squeezing pressure with your legs to avoid getting reversed.

I hook the crook of my right knee over my left foot to trap Beach in a reverse triangle. I also hook my right arm underneath his right arm. It is important to notice that I have my right foot buried in Beach's belly. This not only helps pin him to the ground, but it also prevents him from turning into me and breaking my hold.

I latch onto Beach's right arm with both hands, and then I flatten him out by rolling to my back.

Having forced Beach flat on his back, I bring my left leg out from underneath my right leg, and I then maneuver my left leg over his head.

I drop my left leg down on Beach's face. To finish the armlock, I pull Beach's right arm to my chest, squeeze my legs tight, and elevate my hips.

ARM BAR FROM BACK

If your opponent is an expert at defending against the rear naked choke, catching him in an arm bar is an excellent alternative. As you can see in the photos below, you want to lock one of your opponent's arms up as if you are going for a kimura. Then you slide your arm over his head, pivot out to the side, and throw your leg over his head to lock in the submission. Obtaining the kimura lock is a very important step because it allows you to keep your opponent from bridging and stealing the top position.

I have taken Beach's back. I'm sitting up behind him, my right arm is underneath his right arm, I am grabbing his right wrist with my right hand, and I have both hooks established.

As I drop my left arm over Beach's left shoulder, I release my right grip on his right wrist. Before he has a chance to pull his right arm away, I re-grab his wrist with my left hand.

I grab my left wrist with my right hand, establishing the Kimura lock.

I place my left foot on Beach's left hip and push off. This allows me to turn my body in a counterclockwise direction and get the angle I need to secure the arm bar.

As I continue to rotate in a counterclockwise direction, I slide my left arm over Beach's head. Notice that my grip has not changed.

Continuing to rotate in a counterclockwise direction, I roll to my back. Notice how my body is now perpendicular to Beach's body. To prevent him from posturing up, I keep my lock on his arm tight and maintain downward pressure with my right leg.

Applying downward pressure with my right leg to prevent Beach from posturing up, I pull my left leg out from underneath his body and bring it over his head.

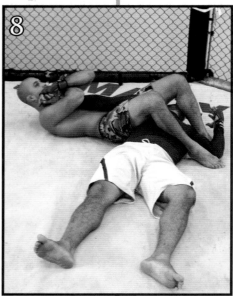

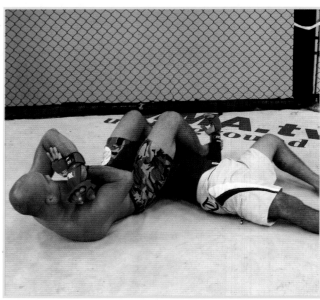

To finish the armlock, I pull Beach's arm to my chest, squeeze my knees together, and elevate my hips.

THE GROUND GAME

BACK TO MOUNT TRANSITION

When you take your opponent's back, expect him to do everything in his power to escape the position. If your opponent is sitting up, he will most likely attempt to slip out to the side and get his back on the canvas. If he can manage this, not only do you no longer have his back, but he can also roll over and end up in your guard. To avoid this, a good option is to grab on to his far shoulder and pull yourself up into the mount as he goes down to his back. I see a lot of fighters who attempt to hopelessly hold on to their opponent's back, and they lose their dominant positioning as a result. It's important to remember that you're not sacrificing positioning by going to the mount—you're just moving from one dominant position to another.

I have taken Paco's back. In addition to having both hooks, I've also established double under-hooks. I accomplished this by sliding my right arm under Paco's right arm and latching onto his shoulder with my right hand, and sliding my left arm under his left arm and latching onto his left wrist with my left hand.

Realizing he is in trouble, Paco begins driving his weight back and to his left in an effort to get both of his shoulders flat to the mat.

Paco drives his weight all the way back and begins to turn into me.

Realizing I have lost Paco's back, I slip out from underneath him and slide my right leg over his body so I can claim the mount.

As I bring my right leg all the way over Paco's body, I move my right arm to the left side of his head.

Posting on my left elbow and knee, I push my body up on top of Paco. As I do this, I maintain downward pressure with my body to prevent Paco from scrambling. It is important to notice that I've trapped his right arm with the right side of my head. This will set me up to apply a choke.

Once on top of Paco, I secure the mount position by sliding my right arm underneath his head, applying downward pressure, and touching my heels together under his legs. From here I am in a perfect position to set up a kata-gatame choke (p. 267).

TURTLE ESCAPE TO STANDING

There are several ways that you can end up in the bottom turtle position. Regardless of how it happens, you want to escape as quickly as possible. A good way to accomplish this is to climb to your feet, move way from your opponent to loosen his hold and prevent him from picking you up, and then break his grip with your hands.

Paco is on my back with a double under-hook body-lock.

Without hesitating, I come up onto my right foot.

Pushing off my right foot, I rise to my feet and immediately wedge both thumbs to the inside of his hands.

To break Paco's grip, I step forward with my right leg, drive my hands toward the ground, lean back, and press my hips forward.

As I break Paco's grip, I pivot in a counter-clockwise direction and continue to back away.

Pivoting around so I'm facing Paco, I assume my fighting stance.

BASIC TURTLE ESCAPES

ROLLING TO GUARD TURTLE ESCAPE

In this technique you execute a forward roll from the bottom turtle position to force a scramble, and the goal of that scramble is to pull your opponent into your guard. You're basically getting the hell out of Dodge before your opponent can throw damaging strikes or establish his hooks and take your back. In order for the technique to work, you must roll over onto the shoulder that is closest to your opponent.

I'm in the bottom turtle position and Paco is working to take my back.

Before Paco has a chance to get his hooks in and secure my back, I roll over onto my left shoulder. Notice that I've rolled over onto the shoulder closest to my opponent. This allows me to get my hips to the outside of his body and roll into the guard position.

Notice how the momentum of my forward roll pushes Paco forward, causing him to struggle to maintain his grip.

As I roll, Paco's grip is broken and he is forced away from me. I use the opportunity to turn my body into him and capture him in my guard.

Continuing to roll onto my shoulders, I elevate my knees to catch Paco in my guard.

I roll all the way over to my back and establish the open guard position.

CHOKE DEFENSE 101

When an opponent has your back, defending your neck should always be your top priority. If you put all of your focus into trying to peel your opponent's hooks off your legs or get your back to the ground, you will most likely get choked and lose the fight. Protecting your neck has to come first. Personally, I like to figure-four my arms around my neck to close up all the gaps that might allow my opponent to sneak an arm around my throat.

To protect my neck from the rear naked choke, I bring my left arm across my neck as if I am trying to choke myself, hook my left palm on top of my right biceps, and then coil my right arm tight against the right side of my head.

Tony attempts to work his arm across my neck to choke me, but my neck is fully protected. All holes are blocked. From here, I will attempt to escape this compromising position by working to get my back to the mat.

BACK AND CHOKE ESCAPE

The worst possible scenario is when your opponent has slapped on a rear naked choke and you feel yourself starting to go out. If you should find yourself in such a pickle, don't panic. The first thing you must do is reach up and grab your opponent's arm that is behind your head because it's how he generates leverage to lock the choke tight. Once you've pulled that arm down, grab the arm that is around your neck, pull it down, and then lift it up and over to the other side of your head. This gives you the ability to drop your back down to the mat and turn around so that you end up in your opponent's guard.

Paco has my back and he's managed to slap on a rear naked choke. In order to escape this fight-ending submission, I need to quickly break his hold.

I reach my left hand up and pull Paco's left arm down. It is important that you remove your opponent's anchor hand from behind your head because it's how he generates leverage to lock in the choke.

I continue to pull Paco's left arm down, and then I straighten it over my left shoulder.

Now that I've eliminated Paco's left arm from the picture, I begin prying his right arm away from my neck using my right hand. It is important to notice that I've turned my head to my left to alleviate pressure from my neck.

Once I pry Paco's right arm away from my neck with my right hand, I double up on his right arm with my hands.

Controlling Paco's right arm with both hands, I begin to maneuver it over to the left side of my head.

I move Paco's right arm to the left side of my head, and I then use both hands to straighten his arm over my left shoulder. This prevents him from being able to maneuver his arm back to the right side of my head and re-secure the choke.

Maintaining downward pressure on Paco's right arm with my hands, I push off my feet and shoot my head back.

Posting on my right foot and pushing off, I continue to drive my head back. At the same time, I reach my right arm up and grip the back of Paco's head with my right hand.

Using my grip on the back of Paco's head for leverage, I twist my body in a clockwise direction. As my torso and hips turn toward the mat, Paco's right hook slips free.

Crawling up to my knees, I pull my left arm out from underneath me and wrap it around Paco's back to secure the top position.

BJ PENN, nicknamed "The Prodigy", was introduced to Brazilian Jiu-Jitsu in Hilo, Hawaii at the tender age of seventeen by neighbor Tom Callos. It was through Tom Callos that BJ met Ralph Gracie in 1997 and decided to relocate to Mountain View, CA to further his jiu-jitsu training. From that time on, Penn launched his storied career through the ranks of Brazilian Jiu-Jitsu and mixed martial arts competition. He is a former UFC Welterweight World Champion, a Mundial World Champion, and one crazy S.O.B.

GLEN CORDOZA is a professional Muay Thai kickboxer and MMA fighter. He is the author of six books on the martial arts.

ERICH KRAUSS is a professional Muay Thai kickboxer who has lived and fought in Thailand. He has written for the New York Times and is the author of seventeen books. His first fiction title, OLEG, will be released in 2008.

Books By Victory Belt (available on www.victorybelt.com)

GRAPPLING by BJ Penn with Erich Krauss & Glen Cordoza
BRAZILIAN JIU-JITSU by BJ Penn with Erich Krauss & Glen Cordoza
WRESTLING FOR FIGHTING by Randy Couture with Erich Krauss & Glen Cordoza
THE X-GUARD by Marcelo Garcia with Erich Krauss and Glen Cordoza
MASTERING THE TWISTER by Eddie Bravo with Glen Cordoza & Erich Krauss
MASTERING THE RUBBER GUARD by Eddie Bravo with Erich Krauss and Glen Cordoza
GUERRILLA JIU-JITSU by Dave Camarillo with Erich Krauss
GUERRILLA JIU-JITSU: FOR MMA by Dave Camarillo with Glen Cordoza & Erich Krauss
MASTERING THE RUBBER GUARD (DVD) by Eddie Bravo & the Victory Belt Staff